World security and equity

World security and equity

Jan Tinbergen
Professor Emeritus of Development Planning
Erasmus University, Rotterdam

Edward Elgar

Published by
Edward Elgar Publishing Limited
Gower House
Croft Road
Aldershot
Hants GUll 3HR
England

Gower Publishing Company
Old Post Road
Brookfield
Vermont 05036
USA

British Library Cataloguing in Publication Data

Tinbergen, Jan
   World security and equity.
   1. International relations. Policies of governments
   I. Title
   303.4'82

Library of Congress Cataloging-in-Publication Data

Tinbergen, Jan, 1903–
   World security and equity / Jan Tinbergen.
     p. cm.
     ISBN 1–85278–187–4.—
     1. Welfare economics — Mathematical models. 2. Economic
security—Mathematical models. 3. National security—
Mathematical models. 4. International cooperation—
Mathematical models. I. Title. HB846. T56 1990
     361.6'1—dc20   89–23686
ISBN 1–85278–187–4   CIP

Printed in Great Britain by
Billing & Sons Ltd, Worcester

Contents

Foreword

This book is an attempt to strengthen the foundations of a book *Warfare and Welfare* which Dietrich Fischer and I published in 1987. It dealt with the integration of security policy and economic policy in the restricted sense. Some of the main points of view were illustrated by quantitative models whose use in the preparation of economic policy is generally accepted. These models are very simple, however, and play a modest role in our main argument. In that book we announced our intention to work out those illustrations of our analysis at a later date in order to strengthen our main thesis. The main conclusions and propositions of *Warfare and Welfare* were given in qualitative and verbal form, dealing mainly with the optimal world decision-making structure.

The present book tries to provide a quantitative foundation, such as is customarily used in policy planning. The novelty of the subject and the restricted data base require a number of alternative approaches. They have in common that the geographical area is either the whole world or at least its most important parts, such as all market economies or the two super-powers or the members of the two main military alliances, NATO and the Warsaw Pact.

Alternatives are also shown with regard to the welfare (or utility) functions. Two types have been used, both showing decreasing marginal utility with increasing quantities consumed – a feature which I believe most economists would require. The difference between the two types is that one does not show satiation and so reflects the long-held philosophy that human needs are unlimited; the other type assumes that they are not nor should they be.

Recently, mankind has been confronted – especially by the Club of Rome – with the fact that the quantities of consumable goods and services annually available are limited and that we may be forced by our environment to accept 'limits to growth'. Already, it is becoming a serious problem how to ensure a decent life for the unlimited *number* of future generations, as distinct from *size*: both require modesty in what we claim for ourselves.

All models dealt with are macro-models, in contrast to some world models developed by others. They are one-man products: micro-models can only be built by institutes. My hope is that some features of my one-man job may be useful in teaching, that is, in making our subject under-standable, or to the builders of micro-models: real policy-making agencies.

It seems to be useful for the readers – and among them the reviewers– of a book for the author to formulate what he claims to be new. The novel elements in this book are, in the author's opinion, the following:

1. The aims of military policy (security) and development co-operation (equity) cannot be pursued independently. Contrary to the opinion of the 1986 American government, they are interrelated, and so it made sense that in 1987 the United Nations organized a meeting of member governments on this interrelationship.
2. The amount of 0.7 per cent of GNP proposed as a norm for Official Development Assistance (ODA) in 1970 should be replaced by a more sophisticated criterion. In this book three are proposed, which have in common that they are considerably higher amounts.
3. ODA should be a percentage of GNP that is higher for high-income donor countries than for lower-income donor countries.
4. In order to maximize world welfare-in-security, reductions in military expenditures of the same order as the increase in development assistance are necessary.
5. More concrete research programmes on the measurement of security levels are proposed.

I want to thank Edward Elgar Publishing Ltd, and in particular Mr Edward Elgar himself, for the interest shown in and help provided for the publication of this book. I also want to thank an anonymous reader for a great number of comments on an earlier version, which substantially contributed to the clarity of the text. And – again – I want to thank Mrs Suze Kleyngeld for her skill and patience in typing the text which contains so many mathematical formulae and complicated tables.

Jan Tinbergen
The Hague

1. Introduction

1.1 WELFARE; ORGANIZATION OF THE BOOK

In this chapter the main concepts, some of their relevant features and a survey of the models to be developed will be dealt with. In addition, some pioneers in our subject – individuals as well as institutions – and the main data sources will be listed. This is comparable to the list of *dramatis personae* of a play.

The central concept of economic science is welfare. We shall consider the terms 'satisfaction' or 'utility' as identical to welfare. Human beings, individually and in groups, aim at maximizing their welfare within the set of restrictions imposed on them. Restrictions are imposed on them by nature as well as by man-made institutions. Natural restrictions may be the natural environment (for example climate) as well as the personal characteristics of an individual (her or his needs and capabilities). Restrictions by man-made institutions are the individual's rights and duties (for example, old-age pension and payment of taxes or bus fares). Welfare and restrictions both show a large number of components. Welfare has many determinants such as food, clothing and satisfaction from or irritation by work. Restrictions are numerous since human nature, as well as modern society, is complicated.

In macro-economic models the complicated character of both welfare and the restrictions is almost hidden by the use of complicated macro-economic concepts for welfare's determinants (for instance, total consumer expenditure) and for restrictions (for instance, national income plus foreign assistance as the restriction on all expenditures). In Sections 1.4 to 1.6 inclusive welfare functions will be specified, that is, how welfare depends on its determinants.

With their aid a number of different problems will be formulated which constitute aspects of the subject of this book. This subject may be briefly described as how to maximize world security and equity and was dealt with by Dietrich Fischer and the present author in our book *Warfare and Welfare* (Fischer and Tinbergen, 1987) in a non-mathematical way. As an illustration, only three models of a mathematical character were discussed, but the general argument was verbally presented. It is the purpose of the present book to extend and, hopefully, to reinforce the foundations of the 1987 book by the discussion of a large number of models. A survey of these models will be given in Section 1.7. The formulation and treatment of the models constitutes the main part of the book, set out in Chapters 2 to 7. Chapter 8 brings together the main conclusions attained with the aid of the ten groups of models studied, most of them containing several alternative specifications. Section 1.8 of the present chapter (Appendix I) informs the reader on the history of world modelling. Section 1.9 (Appendix II) lists the sources of data.

1.2   SECURITY

In our 1987 book Professor Fischer and I argued that security policy affects welfare, the conventional objective of socio-economic policy, to such an extent that the two policies had better be integrated. This is particularly true as a consequence of the existence of nuclear weapons, but it can also be argued to be a consequence of what was called 'total war' in the Second World War and even of the tremendous human suffering already experienced in the First World War. The integration of security policy and conventional economic policy implied that the aim of such a generalized economic policy becomes 'welfare in security' or 'generalized welfare'.

The concept of security, we stated, is important in its own right, but on superficial inspection, underdeveloped nevertheless. Textbooks of international law such as Röling's (Röling, 1985) or the Report of the Palme Commission (Palme *et al.*, 1982, 1986) are not clear about its nature, and a generally accepted definition and a method to measure security does not yet exist. The attempt presented in this book does not reflect a generally accepted definition but just an attempt submitted. It weakly reflects some of Röling's suggestions. The empirical research suggested in *Warfare and Welfare* has not started yet. The approach followed in this book is that security's determinants or components are considered to be military expenditures and expenditures on some non-military goods, services or information. Both categories may be subdivided into numerous components, but the only subdivision made in this book is into defensive and offensive military expenditures. Examples of security-relevant non-military expenditures are supplies of grain or of high technology for peaceful uses. An important aspect of security expenditures is how decisions on them are made: by sovereign nations or in various forms of co-operation or co-ordination between sovereign nations.

1.3 OPTIMAL WELFARE IN SECURITY; SECURITY AND DEVELOPMENT AID; 'WORLDS' DISTINGUISHED; WORLD DECISION-MAKING STRUCTURE

The aim of the policies or of the political institutions to be discussed is 'optimal' welfare in security, that is, its maximum value possible within the framework of the restrictions imposed on the decision makers. Some possible restrictions were mentioned in Section 1.1. Aims have to be attained by using the means chosen by the decision makers. Means are phenomena controlled by the latter, such as the set of institutions of the socio-economic order. An essential difference exists between the Western world and the Eastern, communist-ruled world. Another terminology calls them market economies and centrally planned economies. Quantitative means, such as taxes or subsidies, will be called instruments. Military and non-military expenditures are examples already mentioned. Non-military expenditures for security aims may be called security assistance or aid, comparable with development aid as a policy instrument in development co-operation. Security assistance is an instrument used by countries of the First World (W1) in their relationship with the Second (communist-ruled) World (W2), whereas development assistance is used by W1 in its relation with the Third World (W3). In a large number of our models the world as a whole is subdivided in this highly 'macro' way. The world as a whole is also sometimes subdivided even more simply: W1 and W2 are considered 'developed', W3 'underdeveloped' (or 'developing'). An alternative subdivision is in 'market economies' (W1 + W3) and 'centrally planned' (W2). A clear case of doubt, to be discussed, is where China (with one quarter of the world population) has to be located. There are several more doubtful cases, such as Vietnam or Portugal. Whenever in a model the maximization of some variable (mostly welfare-in-security) or some other target is aimed at, a decision-making structure is implied that enables the policy makers concerned to implement that target. We shall call this aspect the 'world decision-making structure'. The structure at stake may be the existence of treaties between sovereign nations, by the existence of supranational authorities for a limited area (such as the European Community) or for the world at large. Its competence may cover a few or a large number of fields of activity, and so on.

This structure is dealt with extensively in Dietrich Fischer's and my book *Warfare and Welfare* (op. cit.). Here the emphasis is on the quantitative aspect of the decisions; and the decision-making structure is, as a rule, implicitly related to the targets set and the values of the instrument variables found (if the value is nil, no decision-making institution is needed).

1.4   WELFARE FUNCTIONS; DIMINISHING MARGINAL UTILITY

To begin with, the analysis is made in the simplest way possible, that is, using the smallest number of actors necessary to deal with our problems. This requires at least one actor each for the First, Second and Third Worlds. Each of these actors' roles is based on his welfare-in-security, and is dealt with in the same way as individual actors in micro-economic theory. Later (Chapters 5 and 6), a larger number of actors, down to single nations, will be introduced.

Our assumption is that the welfare function characterizes the human race, and hence is the same for all human beings. It depends on human properties, such as intelligence, and therefore schooling, however. These act as parameters. For lack of data we neglect these aspects in the most macro chapters (1 to 4 inclusive). A better specification is offered in Section 6.3.

Welfare-in-security (or generalized welfare, or just utility, used as synonyms) is assumed to be measurable, following recent trends in economic science (cf. Tinbergen, 1985 and 1987). A functional relationship is assumed between utility ω and its determinants. Two main types of utility functions are used. Both satisfy the 'law of diminishing marginal utility'. If there is only one determinant, expenditure e, one type used is:

$$\omega = \ln (e + 1) \qquad (1.41)$$

The corresponding marginal utility is

$$\frac{\partial \omega}{\partial e} = \frac{1}{e + 1} \qquad (1.42)$$

and this is falling for rising values of e. For $e = 0$ utility, $\omega = 0$ and for rising values of e utility rises without any limit. Van Praag and his school opted for a lognormal utility function, which does not show diminishing marginal utility. Van Herwaarden and Kapteyn (1981) presented an empirical comparison of the shape of welfare functions and concluded that 'the logarithmic function performs slightly, though significantly, better' than the lognormal and eleven other shapes. The determinant used by these authors is income. Our first determinant will be total expenditure on non-military goods and services, which is closely connected with income.

In the models in this book at least one more determinant will often be introduced, for instance, military expenditure a. Then it is assumed that welfare is:

$$\omega = \ln (y + 1) + \alpha \ln (a + 1) \tag{1.43}$$

where y is non-military spending and a is military expenditure. Evidently α is a measure of the relative preference for military expenditure.

1.5 SATIATION

The logarithmic utility function assumes that an increase in expenditure will always result in increased generalized welfare. It reflects the often-defended view that human needs have no limit. This is not correct in the case of the need for individual goods or services. It is common experience that such need shows satiation and even oversatiation. It is less clear whether this also applies to total expenditure, since the number of goods and services has increased without limit and is invented by technological research and sold with the aid of advertizing. For good reasons this imposition of the purchase of ever-increasing numbers of goods is some-times described as the creation of 'artificial' needs. The limits of real, as compared with artificial, needs are unclear. As an ethical principle the assumption of satiation for total expenditures deserves support in a world where very many individuals suffer from too low incomes even to satisfy their basic needs. Therefore, we are going to study the consequences of utility functions showing satiation and oversatiation as an alternative to the utility functions mentioned in Section 1.4. This seems to make sense, in particular with regard to military expenditure: the existence of the tremen-dous overkill capacity of today's arsenals is a convincing argument in favour of this assumption. For general expenditure it seems not very realistic.

1.6   A PARABOLIC WELFARE FUNCTION

The simplest mathematical shape of a utility function that combines decreasing marginal utility with the existence of satiation and oversatiation is a parabolic utility function:

$$\omega = \omega_0 - \frac{\omega_0}{y_0^2} (y - y_0)^2 + \alpha\omega_0 - \frac{\alpha\omega_0}{a_0^2} (a - a_0)^2 \quad (1.61)$$

In it two determinants have been assumed to occur: non-military (y) and military (a) expenditure. In the case of one determinant we have two parameters y_0 and ω_0 where y_0 is the value of y for which ω is a maximum and ω_0 the maximum value of ω. For $y > y_0$ utility decreases; so y_0 is the satiation value and beyond y_0 there is oversatiation. For $y = 2y_0, \omega = 0$. For national averages y will be below y_0 even for wealthy countries, at least according to public opinion in these countries. Another question is whether inhabitants of poor countries think so too. To them, rich countries' y may surpass what poor countries' public opinion thinks about y_0. This question may be an interesting subject for inquiries by public opinion polls. For the elaboration of world co-operation policies such information might be relevant. Whereas social policy rightly emphasizes the usefulness of information on a minimum income needed to satisfy basic needs, a world social policy may have to study also which values of y_0, the 'satiation income level', are necessary to guarantee a world-wide minimum income.

For the study of arms-control policies information on a_0 is relevant. Values of a_0 are different, of course, under different regimes of international security policy. Under an optimal world security regime, present values of a are definitely larger than a_0. A utility function may contain a logarithmic term for y and a parabolic term for a, such as:

$$\omega = \ln (y + 1) + \omega_0 - \frac{\omega_0}{a_0^2} (a - a_0)^2 \quad (1.62)$$

1.7   SURVEY OF MODELS USED

As announced, the main part of this book consists of a considerable number of studies of an optimal welfare-in-security policy or order, based on a series of macro-economic models. With their aid either the complete problem of the world's security and development or its main components, a security policy and a development policy, are analyzed. These analyses may be grouped according to their main characteristics. One characteristic is whether the model used is *static or dynamic*. The larger part (Chapters 2 to 6 inclusive) is based on static models in the sense of Frisch's definition (Frisch, 1929). Static models are not restricted to stationary (constant) values of the variables considered. The variables may change over time, because some exogenous variables of the model show movements, usually monotonous, but occasionally cyclical. The relevant cycles as a rule are long cycles and not juglars or kitchins (cycles with periods of up to about ten years). Chapter 7 deals with some dynamic models in Frisch's sense. In such models at least one variable's value must occur for different time units. The movements of the variables' values are endogenous: they may show movements even if all exogenous variables are stationary. Endogenous movements may be cyclical, but need not be.

A second main characteristic of the models used consists of the *number and the nature of the geographical units considered*, mentioned briefly in Section 1.3. All models are macro-models, but some are 'less macro' than others. Chapters 2, 3 and 4 respectively deal with 2, 3 and 4 geographical units or 'worlds'. Among the worlds considered are the areas known as the First (W1), the Second (W2) and the Third (W3) World. W1 consists of the developed market economies, but sometimes members of NATO only. W2 consists of the developed communist-ruled countries and so practically coincides with the members of the Warsaw Pact, except when China is included (W2', Section 3.1). W3 consists of the underdeveloped market economies, including the newly industrialized countries (NICs). In Section 3.2, however, China is included, because it is a centrally-planned country. Because of its size China is called the Fourth World (W4) in Chapter 4.

So much for the 'very macro' models studied. Chapters 5 and 6 are reserved for two 'less macro' models, both consisting of twenty worlds. The first of these are not twenty geographical areas, but twenty groups of individuals (or households). Ten live in W1 and are the 'deciles' (one-tenth each) of the population, arranged according to income. The first decile is the poorest tenth, the tenth decile constitutes the richest ten per cent. The other ten groups are the deciles in W3.

The second twenty-worlds model does consist of twenty geographical areas in the world's market economies, W1 + W3. Each has a population of about 5 per cent of the total population. Six are developed and fourteen underdeveloped. These data are available thanks to work done by Kravis *et al* (1982).

1.8 APPENDIX I: PIONEERS IN WORLD MODELS

Economic models as a tool for formulating policy proposals have been built and used for half a century, and the jubilee was celebrated in 1987 by a congress held in Amsterdam. The year 1987 also marked the 125th birthday of the Netherlands Economic Association (cf. Knoester, 1987).

It took some time for the model-building profession to devote itself to models with a wider scope. Increasing interdependency of the world's nations made international policies ever more important and this was reflected in a growing series of economic models of the world at large. Probably the first such model was built by J. J. Polak (1953). Another early world model was J. L. Mosak's, used for United Nations' tasks, and in particular for the United Nations Development Planning Committee, created in 1966. At that time the model existed already; unfortunately it was never published. In 1970 the Department of Applied Economics of the Brussels Free University published another world model (Duprez and Kirschen, 1970). In 1976 another Belgian economist J. Waelbroeck edited a collection of national models that had been used by the so-called Project Link (Waelbroeck, 1976). In 1977 W. Leontief and collaborators produced a series of alternative world models (Leontief *et al.*, 1977) in order to forecast the world economy's situation around the year 2000. Important work has also been done in the Science Centre, Berlin, by Professor K.W. Deutsch (cf. Deutsch, 1984) and collaborators.

1.9 APPENDIX II: SOURCES OF PRINCIPAL DATA

The importance of econometric models is to enable theories on the subject studied to be tested with the aid of statistical data. Clearly, much depends on the quality of the statistics used. In the present study extensive use has been made of two publications by Professor I.B. Kravis and his collaborators resulting from a thorough study made under the auspices of the World Bank (Kravis *et al.*, 1978, 1982).

The 1978 article shows *per capita* real incomes (GDP) for more than 100 countries. Real incomes means that the incomes are expressed in (1975) US dollars buying-power, on the basis of very extensive and careful price comparisons. The 1982 publication is the official report on the subject to the World Bank and contains some estimates for the communist countries in addition. The 1978 article also shows a distribution of real incomes over seven geographical areas, used for our twenty-worlds model.

Another source of great importance is Ruth Leger Sivard's annual publication *World Military and Social Expenditures*, of which we selected the 10th anniversary (1985) edition. It contains 1982 figures, in US dollars, for 142 countries, of GNP, military expenditures, population and several other items. One complication is that for non-USA countries the amounts of GNP and military expenditures are expressed in dollars with the aid of exchange rates and not, as Kravis's figures,of purchasing power parities.

A third important source of data were some of E. F. Denison's studies on the components of economic growth in the USA, a number of European countries and Japan, which contain estimates of growth consequent on technological development.

REFERENCES

Denison, E. F. (1967), *Why Growth Rates Differ* (Brookings Institution, Washington, D.C.).

Denison, E. F. (1974), *Accounting for United States Economic Growth* (Brookings Institution, Washington, D.C.).

Deutsch, K. W. (1984), 'Zur Bedeutung von Weltmodellen – Verstehen lernen wie sich die Welt verändert [On the importance of world models – to learn and understand why the world changes]', *WZB-Mitteilungen*, no. 25 (1084), Science Centre Berlin pp. 12–15.

Duprez, C. and E. S. Kirschen (eds) (1970), *Megistos, A World Income and Trade Model for 1975* (North-Holland, Amsterdam and London; American Elsevier, New York).

Fischer, D. and J. Tinbergen (1987), *Warfare and Welfare* (Wheatsheaf Books, Brighton).

Frisch, R. (1929), Statikk og dynamikk i den økonomiske teori [Statics and dynamics in economic theory]', *Nationaløkonomisk Tidsskrift*, pp. 229–72.

Knoester, A., (ed.) (1987), *Lessen uit het verleden* [Lessons from the Past] (H. E. Stenfert Kroese B.V. Leiden, Antwerpen).

Kravis, I. B. *et al.* (1978), 'Real GDP *Per Capita* for More than One Hundred Countries', *Economic Journal*, vol. 88 no. 350, pp. 215–42.

Kravis, I. B. *et al.* (1982), *World Product and Income. International Comparison of Real Gross Product* (Johns Hopkins University Press, Baltimore and London, for the World Bank).

Leger Sivard, Ruth (1985), *World Military and Social Expenditures* (World Priorities, Washington, D.C.)

Leontief, W. *et al.* (1977), *The Future of the World Economy, A United Nations Study* (Oxford University Press, New York).

Palme, O. *et al.* (1982, 1986), *Common Security. A Blueprint for Survival*, by the Independent Commission on Disarmament and Security Issues (Simon and Schuster, New York (1982) and Delhi (1986)).

Polak. J. J. (1953), *An International Economic System* (University of Chicago Press, Chicago, and George Allen and Unwin, London).

Röling, B. V. A. (1985), *Volkenrecht en Vrede* [International Law and Peace] (Kluwer, Deventer).

Tinbergen, J. (1985), 'Measurability of Utility (or Welfare)', *De Economist*, vol. 133, pp 411–14.

Tinbergen, J. (1987), 'Measuring Welfare of Productive Consumers', *De Economist*, vol. 135, pp. 231–6.
Van Herwaarden, F. G. and A. Kapteyn (1981), 'Empirical Comparison of the Shape of Welfare Functions', *European Economic Review*, vol. 15 pp. 261–86.
Waelbroeck, J. L. (ed.)(1976), *The Models of Project Link* (North Holland, Amsterdam, New York and Oxford).

2. Two-worlds models

2.1 EAST-WEST MODELS: LOGARITHMIC UTILITY

As announced, Chapters 2 to 4 inclusive will deal with a number of macro-models to be used to estimate the optimal amounts of military and non-military expenditure, of security aid and of development aid. Military expenditures and security aid are mainly a problem of W1 and W2, whereas development aid is mainly a problem of W1 and W3. Since the opinion has been expressed that the two problems are not connected, in the present chapter they will be treated separately. In Chapters 3 and 4 they will be integrated in order to find out whether such integration changes the outcomes.

Two models of the East-West problem will be considered: (W1W2, 1) where only one type of armament is considered, and (W1W2, 2) where two types are considered. The variables of the models are:

n_1, n_2 : population of W1 and W2 ($n_1 = 1$)
x_1, x_2 : national product of W1 and W2 (considered given)
y_1, y_2 : non-military expenditures of W1 and W2
a_1, a_2 : military expenditures (on offensive arms if defensive arms are also considered)
b_1, b_2 : military expenditures on defensive arms (not considered in Model (W1W2, 1))
v_{12} : non-military security assistance from W1 to W2.

The models' equations consist, first of all, of the restrictions. These are the balance equations:

$$x_1 = y_1 + a_1 + b_1 + v_{12} \tag{R1}$$
$$x_2 = y_2 + a_2 + b_2 - v_{12} \tag{R2}$$

where the terms b_1 and b_2 only appear in Model (W1W2, 2).

The other equations express that the unknown variables maximize welfare-in-security. Two problems will be considered, of which Problem I in two versions (I_1 and I_2). In the latter, W1 and W2 are supposed to be

11

sovereign. In that situation v_{12} will be assumed to be negligible ($v_{12}=0$), and W1's welfare maximized under R1.

As the welfare function we first consider the logarithmic function; later the parabolic function will be taken up. So in Problem I_1 we maximize:

$$\omega_1 = \ln (y_1 + 1) + \alpha_{11}\ln (a_1 + 1) + \lambda_1(x_1 - y_1 - a_1) \qquad (2.11)$$

where λ_1 is a Lagrange multiplier and in parentheses what remains of R1 if $b_1 = v_{12} = 0$: then R1 reduces to $x_1 - y_1 - a_1 = 0$ (R1')
The additional equations are maximum conditions for the two unknown variables y_1 and a_1:

$$1/(y_1 + 1) - \lambda_1 = 0 \qquad\qquad (2.12)$$
$$\alpha_{11}/(a_1 + 1) - \lambda_1 = 0 \qquad\qquad (2.13)$$

From (2.12) and (2.13) we derive:

$$a_1 + 1 = \alpha_{11} (y_1 + 1) \qquad\qquad (2.14)$$

Elimination of y_1 with the aid of (R1') yields:

$$a_1 (1 + \alpha_{11}) = \alpha_{11}x_1 + \alpha_{11} - 1 \qquad\qquad (2.15)$$

The smallness of $\alpha_{11} - 1$ in comparison to $a_1 (1 + \alpha_{11})$ enables us to simplify (2.15) into

$$a_1 = \alpha_{11}x_1/(1 + \alpha_{11}) \qquad\qquad (2.16)$$

Since a_1 and x_1 are observed, (2.16) permits us to estimate α_{11}. Using Leger Sivard's figures for 1982, in billion US \$ we have for NATO: $x_1 =$ 6156, $a_1 = 311$ and $\alpha_{11} = 0.053$; and for the USA: $x_1 = 3057$, $a_1 = 196$ and $\alpha_{11} = 0.069$.

In the same way we can solve Problem I_2 and find for the Warsaw Pact: $x_2 = 2084$, $a_2 = 187$ and $\alpha_{22} = 0.099$. For the Soviet Union: $x_2 = 1563$, $a_2 = 107$ and $\alpha_{22} = 0.122$. Here α_{11} stands for the portion of national income spent on armament in the USA and NATO, and α_{22} applies to the Warsaw Pact and the Soviet Union. They are close to the observed figures.

Turning now to Problem II: in order to find the optimal level of armament in a Treaty between East and West, we use (R1) and (R2), putting $b_1 = b_2 = 0$ and maximize

$$\Omega = \omega_1 + \omega_2 = \ln(y_1 + 1) + \alpha'_{11} \ln(a_1 + 1) - \alpha'_{12} \ln(a_2 + 1) +$$
$$0.65 \ln(y_2 + 0.65) + 0.65 \, \alpha'_{22}\ln(a_2 + 0.65) - 0.65 \, \alpha'_{21}\ln(a_1 + 0.65)$$
$$+\lambda_1 (x_1 - y_1 - a_1 - v_{12}) + \lambda_2 (x_2 - y_2 - a_2 + v_{12})$$

The maximum conditions are:

$$1/(y_1 + 1) - \lambda_1 = 0 \qquad\qquad 0.65/(y_2 + 0.65) - \lambda_2 = 0$$
$$-\lambda_1 + \lambda_2 = 0 \qquad\qquad\qquad (2.17)$$
$$\alpha'_{11}/(a_1 + 1) - 0.65 \, \alpha'_{21}/(a_1 + 0.65) - \lambda_1 = 0$$
$$-\alpha'_{12}/(a_2 + 1) + 0.65 \, \alpha'_{22}/(a_2 + 0.65) - \lambda_2 = 0$$

In the expression for Ω, α'_{12} represents the impact of W2's armament on W1 and α'_{21} the impact of W1 armament on W2. The figure 0.65 is the population of W2 in terms of W1, and its appearance in ω_2 is explained in Appendix I. Equation (2.17) results from differentiation of Ω with respect to v_{12}.

For the solution of the system of equations a good approximation will be used for values of $a_1 \gg 1$, $a_2 \gg 1$:

$$\alpha'_{11}/(a_1 + 1) - 0.65 \, \alpha'_{21}/(a_1 + 0.65) \simeq (\alpha'_{11} - 0.65 \, \alpha'_{21})/(a_1 + 0.825)$$
$$(2.18)$$

In the expression for Ω we used the symbols α'_{ij}, $(i, j = 1, 2)$ instead of α_{ij} in order to express that in Problem II, where the two parties are co-operating in some form (for example by a treaty), their need for armament will be smaller than without such co-operation. They need armament to defend themselves against possible aggression by outsiders and against deviation from the treaty by the other party. In all probability this need for arms will be lower than before. Disregarding, to begin with, this effect of co-operation, we stick to the value found for α_{11} and α_{22} and ask ourselves what value α_{12} and α_{21} may have. As far as the weapons are defensive these values may be 0, but since most of them are offensive, they may be of the order of, respectively, α_{22} and α_{11} of which the values were found in the solution of Problems I_1 and I_2. So we think it proper to assume that:

$$0 \le \alpha_{12} \le \alpha_{22} \text{ (0.099 for NATO, 0.122 for the US)}$$
$$0 \le \alpha_{21} \le \alpha_{11} \text{ (0.053 for the WP, 0.069 for the SU)}$$

But there are additional restrictions, because the maximum conditions

(2.17), after elimination of the λ_1 and λ_2 reduce to:

$$\frac{\alpha'_{11} - 0.65\ \alpha'_{21}}{a_1 + 0.825} = \frac{0.65\ \alpha'_{22} - \alpha'_{12}}{a_2 + 0.825}$$
$$= \frac{1}{x_1 - a_1 - v_{12} + 1} = \frac{0.65}{x_2 - a_2 + v_{12} + 1} \qquad (2.19)$$

These equations constitute three equations for the three unknowns a_1, a_2 and v_{12}. The numerators of the first two fractions must be positive. For α_{21} this has no implications, but for α_{12} it imposes lower upper limits, namely 0.65 α_{22}, which for the WP means 0.064 and for the SU 0.079. So for α_{12} we have

$$0 \le \alpha_{12} \le \begin{cases} 0.064 \ \ (\text{WP}) \\[2mm] 0.079 \ \ (\text{SU}) \end{cases}$$

The preceding statements about the lower and upper limits of α_{12} and α_{21} enable us to find lower and upper limits of the numerators of the first two fractions of (2.19). The results are shown in Table 2.11, where we apply the lower and upper values found for the α and the α'.

Table 2.11   *Maximum and minimum values of numerators of 1st and 2nd*
             fractions in (2.19)

		NATO/WP	US/US
1st numerator	maximum	0.093	0.069
	minimum	0.019	0.024
2nd numerator	maximum	0.064	0.079
	minimum	0	0
Average of 4 values		0.034	0.043

Finally, it seems appropriate to assume that $a_1 = a_2 = a$ ('equal strength'), which requires equality of the two numerators, for which we take the averages. The values then obtained for a and v_{12} are shown in Table 2.12.

Table 2.12 *Optimal values for military expenditure a, compared with 1982 values, and security assistance* v_{12} *(billion US$ of 1982)*

	a		v_{12}
	opt.	1982	
NATO/WP	162	311	1197
US/SU	114	196	281

As observed, these figures, 162 and 114, are overestimated, since the α'_{11} and α'_{22} presumably are lower than the α_{11} and α_{22} used in the computations. Interesting research remains to be done, but a reduction by about 50 per cent of military expenditure seems close to an optimum. In addition, large amounts of 'security aid' or non-military security expenditures, 10 or 20 per cent of x_1, are found to be optimal; so large, indeed, as to require explanation. This will be discussed in Section 2.2.

2.2 INTERPRETATION OF THE FINDING OF HIGH FIGURES OF SECURITY AID

The unrealistically high figures found for optimal security aid constitute a problem that we shall face again when development aid is studied (Section 2.5 and beyond). For an appropriate interpretation of our findings it needs careful study. One aspect is that the seriousness of the problems studied (the need for arms reduction and for more development co-operation) is underestimated by many citizens and politicians. Another aspect, however, is that the models used are static models and as a rule the optima found are long-term optima. This aspect may be eliminated by replacing the models by dynamic models and in Chapter 7 this will be done. It deprives us of the simplicity and the clarity of the models, however, and so of their persuasive power. This is why, in the present section, another way of interpreting our results will be offered. The explanation seems to us to be that welfare is assumed to depend on instantaneous expenditure y_1 (mainly consumption) only, and not on any downward change in y_1. A sudden reduction in y_1 as a consequence of security aid has not been taken into account. This implies that we implicitly assumed this reduction to take place in such a way as to avoid a sudden reduction in y_1. This can be arranged by an annual buildup of security aid from the increase of production. This annual increase was, around 1970, 4.15 per cent for W1's production x_1. For NATO it takes less than four years for the fall in a_1 plus the increase in x_1 (= 6156) to become 1197, the optimum of v_{12}. During these four years only what remains after the initial y_1 and the optimal armament have been paid for is available for security aid. These amounts are shown in Table 2.21.

Table 2.21   National product x_1*, armament expenditure* a_1*, non-military expenditure* y_1 *and security aid* v_{12} *of NATO for years 0 to 5 (bnUS$)*

$t =$	0	1	2	3	4
x_1	6156	6411	6678	6955	7243
a_1	311	162	162	162	162
y_1	5845	5845	5845	5845	5845
v_{12}	0	404	671	948	1236
v_{12} as per cent of x_1	0	6.3	10.0	13.6	17.1

The value of y_1 is kept constant and v_{12} is financed out of the rise in x_1, which in year 1 is $6411 - 6156 = 255$; since a_1 is reduced to 162, $311 - 162 = 149$ is available from that source, so in total $255 + 149 = 404$. Security assistance v_{12} will reach its optimum shortly before year 4.

From it we see that, under the assumptions made, in the years 1 to 4 inclusive the percentage of national income spent on 'security aid' will only gradually rise to 17.1. This interpretation enhances the credibility of our results. This method will be described again in Section 2.5, where development aid is discussed, a subject more often debated than security aid.

Table 2.21 is based on income figures $x_1 = 6156$, obtained with the aid of official exchange rates for non-USA countries. Since it is better to use purchasing power exchange rates, as done by Kravis *cum suis* we add Table 2.22 where Kravis's figures have been used, for real incomes and expenditures:

Table 2.22 *National product* x_1, *armament expenditures* a_1, *non-military expenditure* y_1 *and security aid* v_{12} *of NATO for years 0 to 3 (bn 1965 US$)*[1]

$t =$	0	1	2	3
x_1	2406	2506	2610	2718
a_1	122	71.6	71.6	71.6
y_1	2284	2284	2284	2284
v_{12}	0	150.4	254.4	362.4
v_{12} as % of x_1	0	6.0	9.7	13.3

[1]Calculated the same way as Table 2.21

Of course, a more satisfactory method to deal with this approach is one of a dynamic model (cf. Chapter 7).

These are 1975 dollar figures, however, which explains the large part of the deviation from the figures in Table 2.21. Using the Kravis figures we find optimal $a_1 = 71.6$ and $v_{12} = 204.3$ or 8.49 per cent of NATO $x_1 = 2406$. The optimal armament level is well below the 1975 level of 122. Introducing again a gradual buildup of v_{12} we now need somewhat less than 2 years only.

2.3   EAST-WEST MODELS: TWO TYPES OF ARMS

As announced in Section 2.1, models with two types of armament (W1W2,2) have also been studied. Although not all weapons can be strictly classified into offensive and defensive weapons, the classification plays a predominant role already in the discussion of the Anti-Ballistic Missile (ABM) Treaty of 1972 and, again, in the discussion about the Strategic Defence Initiative (SDI).

As an example with crude figures only, we choose a model dealing with the two superpowers (US and SU) and with figures rounded to multiples of 25:

$$x_1 = 2500 \qquad x_2 = 1250$$
$$a_1 = 150 \qquad a_2 = 150$$
$$b_1 = 25 \qquad b_2 = 25$$
$$y_1 = 2325 \qquad y_2 = 1075$$

These figures reflect the lower national product of the SU, the equal level of armament and the minor role played by defensive weapons. We restrict ourselves to the use of logarithmic welfare-cum-security functions. For Problem I, we choose

$$\omega_1 = \ln(y_1 + 1) + \alpha_{11}\ln(a_1 + 1) + \beta_{11}\ln(b_1 + 1)$$

and the restriction: R1: $x_1 = y_1 + a_1 + b_1$
From the optimum conditions we derive:

$$a_1 + 1 = \alpha_{11}(y_1 + 1) \qquad \text{and hence}$$
$$\alpha_{11} = (a_1 + 1)/(y_1 + 1) = 151/2326 = 0.065$$

$$b_1 + 1 = \beta_{11}(y_1 + 1) \qquad \text{and}$$
$$\beta_{11} = (b_1 + 1)/(y_1 + 1) = 26/2326 = 0.011$$

Similarly for the SU, Problem I_2 yields

$$\alpha_{22} = (a_2 + 1)/(y_2 + 1) = 0.140 \text{ and } \beta_{22} = (b_2 + 1)/(y_2 + 1) = 0.024$$

Problem II, where a joint optimum is searched for, requires the introduction of the impact of each power's armament on the welfare-cum-security of the other power and the maximization of:

$$\Omega = \omega'_1 + \omega'_2 = \ln(y_1 + 1) + \alpha'_{11}\ln(a_1 + 1) + \beta'_{11}\ln(b_1 + 1) - \alpha'_{12}\ln(a_2 + 1)$$
$$+ \beta'_{12}\ln(b_2 + 1) + \ln(y_2 + 1) + \alpha'_{22}\ln(a_2 + 1) + \beta'_{22}\ln(b_2 + 1) - \alpha'_{21}\ln(a_1 + 1)$$
$$+ \beta'_{21}\ln(b_1 + 1) + \lambda_1(x_1 - y_1 - v_{12} - a_1 - b_1) + \lambda_2(x_2 - y_2 + v_{12} - a_2 - b_2)$$

Here α'_{ij} constitutes the impact of j's armament on i's welfare and similarly for β'_{ij}. Offensive weapons are supposed to have a negative impact on the other power. Moreover an amount of 'security aid' v_{12} may be agreed upon, flowing from 1 to 2, together with the negotiations on armament reductions. We assume that the two nations want to keep their armament in both categories at the same level, $a_1 = a_2 = a$ and $b_1 = b_2 = b$. The ordinary Lagrange procedure after elimination of λ_1 and λ_2 leads to:

$$y_1 = y_2 = y$$
$$2(a + 1) = (\alpha'_{11} + \alpha'_{22} - \alpha'_{12} - \alpha'_{21})(y + 1)$$
$$2(b + 1) = (\beta'_{11} + \beta'_{22} + \beta'_{12} + \beta'_{21})(y + 1)$$

Direct observations of the 'mixed' coefficients α'_{12}, α'_{21}, β'_{12} and β'_{21} are not available. As long as no direct observations are available we shall use some alternative values satisfying the plausible conditions that $\alpha'_{12} + \alpha'_{21}$ $< \alpha'_{11} + \alpha'_{22} = 0.205$ and $\beta'_{12} + \beta'_{21}$ are of the same order of magnitude as $\beta'_{11} + \beta'_{22} = 0.035$. The first assumption is plausible since it leads to positive values of a, and the second constitutes an upper limit to b; a possible lower limit may be $\beta'_{12} + \beta'_{21} = 0$. The assumptions made and results obtained are shown in Table 2.31. For the reasons mentioned the figures indicate orders of magnitude rather than exact figures. Those orders of magnitude are instructive, and surprisingly differ from what many experts would have expected. This applies to the possible role of security assistance in particular and perhaps to the desirable shift towards defensive arms.

Table 2.31   *Coefficients assumed and optimum values of variables obtained*

	Case (i)	Case (ii)	Case (iii)
α_{11}	←	0.065	→
α_{22}	←	0.140	→
α_{12}	0.05	0.06	0.04
α_{21}	0.10	0.12	0.08
β_{11}	←	0.011	→
β_{22}	←	0.024	→
β_{12}	0.010	0.008	0.014
β_{21}	0.020	0.015	0.030
y	1771	1758	1735
a	48	67	73
b	57	50	68
v_{12}	←	625	→

The results share with previous results the strong redistribution of civilian expenditure y, mainly obtained with the aid of a high value of v_{12}. The particular topic dealt with here is, however, the distribution over defensive and offensive weapons and the total level of military expenditure. In the cases shown a clear shift from offensive to defensive armament is found, even if the values for b are overestimated. Total military expenditures $a + b$ are significantly lower than in the observed situation, where sovereign decisions are made.

The very high value of v_{12} reflects the real income differences between the US and the SU. As soon as the optimum is defined by optimal welfare, income redistribution is the answer. In reality this will not be claimed by the SU; rather they will try to raise their own productivity. A much more modest amount of security aid may be a matter for negotiation, as a *quid pro quo* for some concession, and in the form of the supply of grain or of high technology.

2.4   EAST-WEST MODELS: PARABOLIC WELFARE

We are now going to introduce the parabolic utility function, in order to present the possibility of satiation or even oversatiation. This utility function for one determinant y_1 (non-military expenditure of World 1) takes the form:

$$\omega_1 = \omega_0 - \frac{\omega_0}{y_{01}^2}(y_1 - y_{o1})^2 \qquad (2.41)$$

where ω_o is the maximum level of satisfaction, attained for $y_1 = y_{o1}$, the level of expenditure where satiation has been attained. The first and the second derivatives are:

$$d\omega_1/dy_1 = -\frac{2\omega_0}{y_{01}^2}(y_1 - y_{o1}) \quad \text{and}$$

$$d^2\omega_1/dy_1^2 = -\frac{2\omega_0}{y_{01}^2}$$

From these expressions we see that indeed for $y_1 = y_{o1}$ this utility function has a horizontal tangent and that that point constitutes a maximum of ω_1.

Total welfare will also depend on armament expenditures of the two worlds under consideration (NATO and WP or, occasionally, the US and the SU). As in Section 2.1, Problems I_1, I_2 and II will be formulated and solved. The new parameters $y_{o1}, y_{o2}, a_{o1}, a_{o2}$ are supposed to be given, but have not, to my knowledge, actually been measured so far. Their estimation from public-opinion polls constitutes an interesting research programme. An additional assumption we shall make is that per person the satiation values of a_1 and a_2 are the same for both parties. We assume that each variable has one satiation value. The main purpose of the present section is to find out what effect changes in satiation values and differences of the satiation values of y_1 and y_2 etc. have on the optimal values.

The data of our problems will first be listed, for NATO and WP (cf. Appendices)

Population: $n_2 = 0.65\ n_1$
'National' product $x_1 = 0.62 \times 3880 = 2406$; $x_2 = 1252$ (1975 US\$bn)
Military expenditures $a_1 = (311/6156) \times 2406 = 122$; $a_2 = (127/2084) \times 1252 = 112$
Satiation values (where numerical assumptions are made): $y_{o1} = 6000$, meaning that NATO citizens don't want more non-military expenditures than 1975 US \$6 trillion:

$$y_{o2} = 0.65 \times 6000 = 3900;\ a_{o1} = 400;\ a_{o2} = 0.65 \times 400 = 260$$

Population figures are for 1982, from Leger Sivard (1985).
Ratio 0.62 of NATO and all Developed countries' GNP from ibid.
Absolute figures 3880 and 1252: from Kravis (1982) (last figure given for WP).
Ratios a/x : from Leger Sivard (1985) in 1982.

Problem I_1 assumes that NATO maximizes

$$\omega_1 = \omega_o - \frac{\omega_o}{y_{o1}^2}(y_1 - y_{o1})^2 + \alpha_{11}\omega_o - \frac{\alpha_{11}\omega_o}{a_{o1}^2}(a_1 - a_{o1})^2$$

subject to restriction (R1) : $x_1 = y_1 + a_1$
This requires $(y_1 - y_{o1})/y_{o1}^2 = \alpha_{11}(a_1 - a_{o1})/a_{o1}^2$
Substituting the data, we get $\alpha_{11} = 0.059$
Similarly the formulation of Problem I_2 yields: $\alpha_{22} = 0.043$.
Problem II – optimizing welfare of NATO and WP together – requires the maximization of:

$$\Omega = v - \frac{\omega_o}{y_{o1}^2}(y_1 - y_{o1})^2 - \frac{\alpha'_{11}\omega_o}{a_{o1}^2}(a_1 - a_{o1})^2$$

$$+ \frac{\alpha'_{12}\omega_o}{a_{o2}^2}(a_2 - a_{o2})^2 -$$

$$0.65\left\{\frac{\omega_o}{y_{o2}^2}(y_2 - y_{o2})^2 - \frac{\alpha'_{22}\omega_o}{a_{o2}^2}(a_2 - a_{o2})^2 + \right.$$

$$\left. \frac{\alpha'_{21}\omega_o}{a_{o1}^2}(a_1 - a_{o1})^2\right\} + \qquad (2.42)$$

$$+ \lambda_1(2406 - y_1 - a_1 - v_{12}) + \lambda_2(1252 - y_2 - a_2 + v_{12})$$

where v_{12} constitutes the 'security aid' transferred by NATO to WP.

The optimum conditions will be derived, first of all, from the assumption of a horizontal-tangent maximum, that is, by assuming that the first derivatives of Ω with regard to the unknown variables y_1, a_1, y_2, a_2 and v_{12} are zero. After elimination of the λ_1 and λ_2 and omitting the common factor ω_0, the conditions are:

$$\frac{2\,(y_1 - y_{o1})}{y_{o2}^2} = \frac{1.3\,(y_2 - y_{o2})}{y_{o2}^2} \tag{2.43}$$

$$\frac{2\,(y_1 - y_{o1})}{y_{o2}^2} = \frac{2\alpha'_{11}\,(b_1 - b_{o1})}{y_{o1}^2} - \frac{1.3\,\alpha'_{21}\,(a_1 - a_{o1})}{y_{o1}^2} \tag{2.44}$$

$$\frac{1.3\,(y_2 - y_{o2})}{y_{o2}^2} = \frac{1.3\alpha'_{22}\,(a_2 - a_{o2})}{y_{o2}^2} - \frac{2\alpha'_{12}\,(a_2 - a_{o2})}{y_{o2}^2} \tag{2.45}$$

For convenience's sake we introduce the positive variables:

$$z_1 = y_{o1} - y_1 \qquad\qquad\qquad z_2 = y_{o2} - y_2$$
$$b_1 = a_{o1} - a_1 \qquad\qquad\qquad b_2 = a_{o2} - a_2$$

This transforms equations (2.43), (2.44) and (2.45) into:

$$2\,z_1 / y_{o1}^2 = 1.3\,z_2 / y_{o2}^2 \tag{2.43'}$$

$$2\,z_1 / y_{o1}^2 = \alpha_1 b_1 / a_{o1}^2 \text{ where } \alpha_1 = 2\alpha'_{11} - 1.3\alpha'_{21}$$
$$= 0.7\alpha'_{11} \tag{2.44'}$$

$$1.3\,z_2 / y_{o2}^2 = \alpha_2 b_2 / a_{o2}^2 \text{ where } \alpha_2 = 1.3\,\alpha'_{22} - 2\,\alpha'_{22} \tag{2.45'}$$

In the last two equations we assumed that $\alpha'_{21} = \alpha'_{11}$ and $\alpha'_{12} = \alpha'_{22}$, which seems plausible for offensive weapons, but should be a matter for empirical research. In order to have the simplest set of solvable equations we add up the two restrictions

$$2406 = y_1 + a_1 + v_{12} \tag{R1}$$
$$1252 = y_2 + a_2 - v_{12} \tag{R2}$$

and obtain $3658 = y_1 + y_2 + a_1 + a_2$ $\qquad\qquad$ (R12)
which leaves us with 4 unknowns y_1, y_2, a_1 and a_2 and 4 equations (2.43), (2.44), (2.45) and (R12). As a numerical illustration we choose the

satiation values $y_{o1} = 0.65 \times 6000 = 3900$; $a_{o1} = 400$; $a_{o2} = 0.65 \times 400 = 260$.
The numerical solutions are (rounded):

$$z_1 = 3965 \quad z_2 = 2587 \quad b_1 = 855 \quad b_2 = 495$$

with which correspond:

$$y_1 = 2035 \quad y_2 = 1393 \quad a_1 = -455 \quad a_2 = 755$$

For each unknown an 'admissable' interval exists . Assuming rational behaviour, we must require the y and a to be smaller than or equal to their satiation values, and larger than the observed values for y_1 and y_2.

For the armament figures in the future we may assume figures down to zero (disarmament). So:

$$2284 \leq y_1 \leq 6000; \quad 1140 \leq y_2 \leq 3900; \quad 0 \leq a_1 \leq 400$$
$$\text{and } 0 \leq a_2 \leq 260.$$

Consequently the solutions for y_1, a_1 and a_2 are inadmissable. The assumptions that the maxima with regard to the a_i ($i = 1, 2$) are horizontal ($\partial\Omega/\partial a_i = 0$; $i = 1, 2$) don't apply. Assuming instead that $a_1 = 0$ and maintaining $\partial\Omega/\partial a_2 = 0$ yields $a_2 = -272$, which leads us to the view that $a_1 = a_2 = 0$ yields the admissable maximum Ω. With the satiation values mentioned *complete disarmament* yields maximum welfare-cum-security.

The solutions for the other variables appear to be

$$y_1 = 2217; \quad y_2 = 1441 \quad \text{and } v_{12} = 189$$

This means that a high security aid be paid by NATO to WP, constituting 7.86 per cent of NATO income 2406. This is partly compensated for by the reduction 122 of armament expenditure. Apart from the increased security a financial loss remains of $189 - 122 = 67$ or 2.8 per cent. For WP countries a financial gain of $189 + 112 = 301$ alongside higher security is the result.

More relevant is, of course, the welfare-cum-security gain. This can be calculated from our utility functions and appears to be 0.08351, with a gain for the WP of 0.10471 and a loss for NATO of 0.02120. Here again the overall optimum appears to imply a gain for WP versus a loss for NATO. The explanation is that, as a consequence of its lower real income *per capita* the WP citizens' marginal utility is higher than NATO's. Our remark at the end of Section 2.3 also applies here.

The optimum as here defined also implies an element of redistribution between East and West. This constitutes an element not so far discussed by either East or West. The higher real income *per capita* in Western compared with Eastern developed countries is due to a variety of causes. Partly it may be due to better natural resources available in the West, partly to a more productive social system. The reforms now under way in the East may raise the productivity.

Depending on some of the data of our example, solutions are also possible which fall inside the admissible intervals of the variables. This will now be shown with the aid of another example.

Instead of the values for the coefficients α_1 and α_2 in equations (2.24') and (2.25') we assume $\alpha_1 = \alpha_2 = 0.1$. Whether such values are realistic can only be judged after a closer study has been made of α_{12} and α_{21}, the coefficients indicating the impact of one side's armament on the other side's security. For defensive weapons this impact may be very different from the impact of offensive weapons. Assuming further $y_{o1} = 2300$, $y_{o2} = 1200$, $a_{01} = a_{02} = 125$, the four equations for y_1, y_2, a_1 and a_2 become, similar to (2.43), (2.44), (2.45) and R12:

$$y_1 - 2300 = 2.3878\ (y_2 - 1200) \tag{2.43'}$$
$$y_1 - 2300 = 0.1\ (a_1 - 125) \tag{2.44'}$$
$$y_2 - 1200 = 0.1\ (a_2 - 125) \tag{2.45'}$$
$$y_1 + y_2 + a_1 + a_2 = 3658 \tag{R12}$$

The solution of the optimum problem now runs:

$$y_1 = 22941.1; \qquad y_2 = 1197.5; \quad a_1 = 66.0 \text{ and } a_2 = 100.3$$

where the values for y_1 and y_2 are within the admissible intervals mentioned and those of the a_i ($i = 1,2$) positive and below the initial figures 122 and 112. From these figures the amount of 'disarmament aid' $v_{12} = 45.9$ follows, a much more realistic figure (1.9 per cent of NATO's national income).

2.5   NORTH–SOUTH MODELS: LOGARITHMIC WELFARE

North–South models are in a way simpler than East–West models. Only one type of good needs to be considered and the main problem is whether a flow of development aid should be directed from North to South, that is, in our notation, from W1 to W3. In some other, economic and non-economic, respects, the problems are more complicated, since the distribution over industries and the sociological differences are much larger. Thanks to the pathbreaking work done by Kravis and his collaborators some of the main difficulties have been reduced. They consist of the large price differences between developed and underdeveloped countries. These enlarge the difference between official parities of currencies and their buying parities. For a comparison of welfare the latter are much more appropriate.

The simplest form of the problem of the optimal level of development aid will be discussed with the aid of the following model, where, first, we use logarithmic utility functions. We consider two 'worlds', W1 and W3 which together are the non-communist world. The data used are Kravis's figures for these worlds' real incomes, expressed in 'milliards' (10^9 called 'billions' by Americans) of US dollars with 1975 buying power: $x_1 = 3880$ and $x_3 = 1999$. Unknowns of the problem are the 'development aid' or 'financial transfers' from W1 to W3, v_{13}, and the total expenditure for these two worlds own consumption and investment, indicated as y_1 and y_3 respectively. The optimum values of the unknowns must satisfy the restrictions

$$x_1 = y_1 + v_{13} \tag{R1}$$
and $\quad x_3 = y_3 - v_{13} \tag{R3}$

and maximize:
$$\Omega = \ln(y_1 + 1) + 2.85 \ln(y_3 + 2.85) + \lambda_1(x_1 - y_1 - v_{13}) + \lambda_2(x_3 - y_3 + v_{13})$$

where 2.85 is the population ratio of W3 to W1. Applying the Lagrange method and eliminating the Lagrangian multipliers λ_1 and λ_2 we are left with:

$$\tag{2.51}$$
$$2.85 \ (y_1 + 1) = y_3 + 2.85 \text{ or } 2.85 \ y_1 = y_3 \tag{2.52}$$

Equations (R1), (R3) and (2.52) yield the unknowns:

$$y_1 = 1527; \quad y_3 = 4352; \quad v_{13} = 2353 \text{ (or 60.6 per cent of } x_1)$$

Here we are faced with the very high figures which we also found, in Section 2.2, for security aid. In fact, the value found here for optimal development aid is even much higher still. Apart from reflecting the enormous welfare gap between W1 and W3 the figure also illustrates the long-term character of the elimination of that gap. Figures due to Summers *et al.* (1984) show that world income inequality hardly changed between 1950 and 1980. Between 1960 and 1979 total income x_1 showed an annual increase of 4.15 per cent and x_3 one of 5.76 per cent. In order to fulfil the optimum condition (2.52) x_1/x_3 should become 0.351. Today it is 1.94. It would take 112 years. This is another way of saying that even the next generation of inhabitants of developing countries will experience hardly any improvement of their living conditions in comparison to those in developed countries.

Applying the method set out in Section 2.2 we may also illustrate our point as follows. In order that development aid be given without reducing the standard of living of the donor countries we can make available the increase in national product which is 4.15 per cent per annum minus the rate of increase of population in the developed countries which over the last decades (1960–83) amounted to 0.91 per cent. The percentage of national income annually available for development aid will then be 3.24 per cent, or, in the first year, 126. This amount will increase by 3.24 per cent and reach the optimal amount of 60.6 per cent in 60.6/4.15 = 14.6 years. The figures in Table 2.51 give some more details.

Table 2.51   Increasing development aid while maintaining the standard of living of the developed countries

Year		0	1	2	3	4	...	14
Production of W1(x_1)		3880	4041	4209	4383	4518	...	6856
Needed by W1		3866	3901	3937	3973	4009	...	4389
Available for	absolute	14	105	199	297	399	...	2467
developm. aid	% of 3880	0.36	3.61	7.01	10.6	13.1	...	63.6

Judging these figures against the background of today's power distribution, most readers will be unable to accept them as realistic. But power relations will not remain what they are now. Moreover, the problem we are studying is the problem of what income distribution will maximize welfare and, as observed before, so eliminate some of the tensions that would develop if inequality of world income distribution remains what it is today.

2.6 NORTH–SOUTH MODELS: PARABOLIC WELFARE

Now we take up the problem of optimum development aid using parabolic utility functions. The latter introduce the satiation levels of y_1 and y_3, y_{o1} and y_{o3}, which introduce an additional problem, namely the possibility to introduce the latter and, in particular, y_{o1} as an instrument of policy instead of an independent variable. We propose to use an 'integrated approach', meaning that we combine the original problem with the use of this new instrument. This 'integrated approach' should not be mixed up with other forms of integration, such as integration of economic and security policy or integrated territories (such as the European Community).

Our problem contains four unknowns, y_1, y_3, y_{o1}, y_{o3} and after having calculated these we are able to determine development aid v_{13}. The data we use are the population ratio $p_3/p_1 = 2.85$ and real products $x_1 = 3880$ and $x_3 = 1999$.

We want to maximize

$$\Omega = -\frac{(y_{o1} - y_1)^2}{y_{o1}^2} - 2.85\frac{(y_{o3} - y_3)^2}{y_{o3}^2} \qquad (2.61)$$

under the restriction (R12) $y_1 + y_3 = x_1 + x_3 = 5879$ (2.62)
Clearly Ω will be a maximum when

$$y_{o1} = y_1 \qquad (2.63)$$

and

$$y_{o3} = y_3 \qquad (2.64)$$

Since we have for the four unknowns only three equations, we have one degree of freedom. This may be used in different ways. One way consists of maximizing instantaneous welfare of the whole 'world' considered, that is W1 + W3, and assuming the same utility function for W1 and W3. It brings us back to equal *per capita* spendable income:

$$y_3/y_1 = 2.85 \qquad (2.65)$$

with the same result as found in Section 2.5 and the same interpretation.

The degree of freedom may also be used to apply an alternative criterion, for instance, that the ratio between y_3 and y_1 or of the *per capita*

y_3 and y_1 which is now about constant, double in a period of twenty years. Such doubling requires an annual increase by 3.5 per cent or

$$y_3/y_1 = (1999/3880) \times 1.035 = 0.5332 \qquad (2.66)$$

This yields $y_1 = 3834.5$; $y_3 = 2044.5$ and $v_{13} = 45.5$ or 1.17 per cent of x_1. Also here, as in Table 2.6, the continuation of the process requires rising amounts of development aid up to the level of 60 per cent of the initial x_1; the only consolation being that, as a percentage of x_1, after 20 years this is 27 per cent.

2.7   THE NEED FOR INTEGRATED MODELS

In this chapter, the problems of disarmament and of development have been treated separately, as if there were no interrelation – an opinion adhered to by the American government around 1986. These separate analyses of the two problems had the advantage that relatively simple models could be used, especially because of the macro-character of these models. We introduced security aid alongside development aid as a useful concept and we introduced two alternative utility functions. We also introduced two types of armament, offensive and defensive. Notwithstanding their pluriform attempts to show the main features of macro-reality, our studies showed some common characteristics worth being highlighted. The most striking result is that the optimal values we found for both security aid and development aid are so much higher than the amounts usually discussed among politicians.

It appeared possible to explain this divergency to a considerable extent. But explaining it does not mean that the values currently discussed are acceptable. They are not. If the world income distribution remains as unequal as it is today, the migration of citizens of the Third World to the First World will drastically increase and cause increasing tensions. We must get accustomed to higher, much higher, figures of development aid if we want to avoid these tensions.

REFERENCES

Kravis, I.B. *et al.* (1982), *World Product and Income*, (World Bank, Baltimore).
Leger Sivard, Ruth (1985), *World Military and Social Expenditures*, (World Priorities, Washington, D.C.).
Summers, R. *et al.* (1984), 'Changes in the World Income Distribution', *Journal of Policy Modeling*, vol. 6, pp. 237–70.

3. Three-worlds models

3.1 THE NEED FOR THREE-WORLDS MODELS: SOME ALTERNATIVES

In Chapter 2 only two-worlds models have been used. The problems of disarmament and development have been treated separately, in the spirit of the opinion of the government of the United States of America concerning the meeting organized by the United Nations on disarmament and development. The United States did not participate since in their government's opinion there is no relationship between disarmament and development. To say the least, and in simple words, this is a remarkable opinion. No complicated analysis is required to understand that what is spent on armament cannot be spent on development. The economic models to be discussed in this chapter describe the relationships between the three worlds of which the global society consists and usually indicated by the terms first, second and third world. Roughly speaking, the first world is the group of non-communist developed (or industrialized) countries, the second world is the group of communist-ruled developed countries and the third world that of the underdeveloped countries. Disarmament is a subject mainly (but of course not exclusively) dealt with by negotiations between the first and the second world. Development co-operation is a subject mainly (but again not exclusively) relevant to the first and the third world. Three-worlds models automatically deal with both subjects simultaneously, and enable us to find out whether there is a relationship between the two and how it looks quantitatively.

A closer look reveals that the three worlds may be defined in somewhat different ways and that a number of alternative definitions are possible, as was stated in Section 1.7 of Chapter 1.

The main choice to be made concerns the position of the world's largest country in population, China. It is a communist-ruled country, but underdeveloped. It may be considered as part of the second or of the third world. It may also be considered in isolation.

A second choice is whether for some problems, such as discussions of security questions, the first world as a whole should be considered or the military organized industrialized countries: the members of the North Atlantic Treaty Organisation (NATO). This problem does not exist for the second world in the restricted sense (without China). All its nations are members of the Warsaw Pact (WP). Table 3.1 lists all alternatives considered in this book.

Table 3.11   Alternative definitions of 'worlds' considered

Definition	Symbol	Variable y symbol
Non-communist developed countries	W1	y_1
Members of NATO	W1'	y'_1
Communist-ruled countries (incl. China)	W2	y_2
Communist-ruled developed countries[1]	W2'	y'_2
Underdeveloped non-communist countries	W3	y_3
All underdeveloped countries (incl. China)	W3'	y'_3
China, when considered separately	W4	y_4

[1]All East-European countries. Yugoslavia not included.

The main statistical data used for these 'worlds' are shown in Appendix II.

3.2   ALTERNATIVE SETS OF CALCULATIONS

In our calculations of optimal security assistance (v_{12}) a positive value for v_{12} was found only when we included China in the second world. For this reason we shall consider first a number of results obtained with W1 and W2, that is, the developed world and the communist world including China. Three sets of calculations have been made which all compare optimum values for the relevant variables for three cases, A, B and C. A deals with security optima negotiated by W1 and W2 only; B deals with development co-operation negotiated by W1 and W3 only, and C deals with simultaneous security and development co-operation negotiated by W1, W2 and W3. The first set of calculations is based on logarithmic utility (welfare-cum-security) functions. The second set is based on parabolic utility functions, assuming that the satiation values have been obtained by observation. The figures are arbitrary figures since no such measurements have in fact been made and have illustrative value only. The third set of calculations are also based on parabolic utility functions, but here the satiation values are those which are optimal for the world at large. As this optimality can be interpreted in different ways, since there are three degrees of freedom, the interpretation has been chosen that W1 and W2 both reduce their armament expenditures to 50 milliards of US dollars with 1975 purchasing power. This means a reduction of military expenditures to less than half the 1975 level. Moreover, it has been assumed that 1 per cent of W1 income (x_1 = 3880) is made available as security assistance, hence v_{12} = 39 milliards of 1975 dollars.

Some of the calculations have been based on alternative assumptions, marked (i) and (ii). Thus, the negotiations between W1 and W2 for the third set of calculations (cf. Table 3.23) have been based on the assumptions that (i') armament expenditures of 50 were sufficient and that *per capita* non-armament expenditures in both areas should be equal (a criterion of equity); alternatively the assumptions just mentioned were made: (ii$'$) armament expenditures restricted to 50 and security assistance of 1 per cent of W1 income x_1 = 3880.

Table 3.21 *Optimal values of the variables when they are the result of (A) maximizing welfare of W1 and W2, (B) maximizing welfare of W1 and W3 and (C) maximizing welfare of W1, W2 and W3. Logarithmic welfare functions. For comparison, D gives 1975 actual figures (bn 1975 US$)*

Variable (bn 1975 $)	A W1W2	B W1W3 (i)	B W1W3 (ii)	C W1W2W3	D
y_1 Non-mil. exp. of W1	2050	1458	1527	1370	3699
y_2 Non-mil. exp. of W2	3792	.	.	2535	1866
y_3 Non-mil. exp. of W3	.	4156	4352	3905	1901
a_1 Milit. exp. of W1	40	167	0	26	167
a_2 Milit. exp. of W2	40	.	.	26	182
a_3 Milit. exp. of W3	.	98	0	59	98
v_{12} Security assistance	1790	.	.	519	0
v_{13} Developm. assistance	.	2255	2353	1964	14

(i) Military expenditures of W1 and W3 as in 1975.
(ii) Full disarmament.

Similarly, the negotiations on development assistance between W1 and

W3 (cf. Table 3.21) have been based on the assumptions that either (i) armament expenditure remains as it was (in 1975) or (ii) that complete disarmament had already been attained.

Tables 3.21, 3.22 and 3.23 show the results of the three sets of optimum calculations just mentioned.

Table 3.22   *Optimal values of the variables when they are the result of (A) maximizing welfare of W1 and W2, (B) maximizing welfare of W1 and W3 and (C) maximizing welfare of W1, W2 and W3. Parabolic welfare functions, where satiation values are assumed to have been measured.[1] For comparison D gives 1975 actual figures (bn 1975 US$)*

		A W1W2	B W1W3		C W1W2W3	D
Variable (bn 1975 US$)			(i)	(ii)		
y_1	Non-mil. exp. of W1	2015	1458	1527	1375	3699
y_2	Non-mil. exp. of W2	3727	.	.	2544	1866
y_3	Non-mil. exp. of W3	.	4156	4352	3918	1901
a_1	Milit. exp. of W1	46	167	0	27	167
a_2	Milit. exp. of W2	134	.	.	36	182
a_3	Milit. exp. of W3	.	98	0	27	98
v_{12}	Security assistance	1819	.	.	537	0
v_{13}	Developm. assistance	.	2255	2353	1946	14

1   By way of example the following satiation values have been taken:
    $y_{01} = 6000$; $y_{02} = 11100$; $y_{03} = 17100$; $a_{01} = 400$; $a_{02} = 740$; $a_{03} = 1140$; i.e., equal *per capita* figures for both y_o and a_o.
(i)   Military expenditures of W1 and W3 as in 1975.
(ii) Full disarmament.

The satiation variables have been defined in Section 1.6 and the choice made for their numerical values in the present section. In Table 3.23 the values 50 chosen for a_1 and a_2 are somewhat more cautious than those found in Table 3.21.

Table 3.23   Optimal values of the variables, when they are the result of (A)
maximizing welfare of W1 and W2, (B) maximizing welfare of
W1 and W3 and (C) maximizing welfare of W1, W2 and W3.
Parabolic welfare functions, where satiation values are chosen so as to maximize world welfare. For comparison D gives
1975 actual figures (bn 1975US$)

		A W1W2		B W1W3		C W1W2W3	D
Variable (bn 1975 US$)		(i')	(ii')	(i)	(ii)		
y_1	Non-mil. exp. of W1	2043	3791	1458	1527	1355	3699
y_2	Non-mil. exp. of W2	3779	2031	.	.	2507	1866
y_3	Non-mil. exp. of W3	.	.	4156	4352	3862	1901
a_1	Milit. exp. of W1	50	50	167	0	50	167
a_2	Milit. exp. of W2	50	50	.	.	50	182
a_3	Milit. exp. of W3	.	.	98	0	98	98
v_{12}	Security assistance	1787	39	.	.	515	0
v_{13}	Developm. assistance	.	.	2255	2353	1961	14

(i')   Degrees of freedom choices: $a_1 = a_2 = 50$ and $y_2 = 1.85\ y_1$ ('equity').
(ii') Degrees of freedom choices: $a_1 = a_2 = 50$ and $v_{12} = 1\%$ of x_1 (3880).
(i)   Military expenditures of W1 and W3 as in 1975.
(ii)   Full disarmament.

3.3   THE RELATIONSHIP BETWEEN DISARMAMENT AND DEVELOPMENT

As stated in Section 3.1, the main purpose of the comparisons made in
Tables 3.21, 3.22 and 3.23 has been to show that a relationship exists
between disarmament and development, contrary to the opinion expressed
by the American government in 1986. In all three tables we see that the
optimal amount of v_{13}, development assistance to the Third World, is lower
in Case C than in Case B, that is, lower if security problems have also to
be taken care of. This result is found in all three tables, each based on
another welfare function – whether logarithmic and without the phenomenon of satiation, or parabolic with satiation or, in the latter case, whether
based on autonomous satiation without an ethical principle, or based on an
ethical principle: maximizing world welfare. (The reader will have under-

stood that the word welfare has been used in its widest sense, including the
security aspect.)

The tables show some additional features worth mentioning. First, they
all show the very high values characteristic for statical models, discussed
at some length in Section 2.2. Next, they also show a clear reduction in
armament expenditure when not fixed in advance (Table 3.23). A third
feature is the extreme sensitivity of security assistance to some of the
parameters of the model. This means that, at least in the model used, small
changes in the relative incomes of W1 and W2 require large shifts in
security assistance, whether up or down. It also means that modest
improvements in W2 productivity – given so much attention by Secretary-
General Gorbachev – may considerably reduce the need for any security
assistance. This finding remains a subject for further study.

3.4   THREE-WORLDS MODELS WITH CHINA IN THE THIRD WORLD

As stated in Section 3.1, all calculations made so far have taken W2 to
include China, because including China in W3 leads to negative security
assistance, which is considered unrealistic. In this final section of Chapter
3 some results obtained with that definition of W3 (indicated by W3') will
be shown. In a way it means considering China underdeveloped in the first
place, rather than communist-ruled.

The evidence will be given in the same form as in Section 3.2, that is,
in tables comparing the results of maximizing, respectively, welfare of
W1W2', W1W3' and W1W2'W3'. Here W2' stands for the Warsaw Pact
countries and W3' for the underdeveloped world including China (cf. Table
3.11). We have restricted ourselves to two welfare functions, those used in
Tables 3.31 and 3.33

In both tables the value of 'security assistance' v_{12} is found to be
negative, meaning literally that such assistance should be flowing from the
communist countries to the western, which does not look realistic. The
correct interpretation rather seems to be that the optimum position is a
boundary value, in this case $v_{12} = 0$. Alternatively, v_{12} may be chosen at \$39
bn (1% of 3880).

Substituting the value 0 of v_{12} for the maximum condition $d\Omega /dv_{12} = 0$
we obtain the correct set of optimum values for all variables. Since one of
the parameters – the coefficient α linking armament expenditures and non-
military expenditures – must be chosen somewhat arbitrarily (< 0.10) we

Table 3.41 *Optimal values of the variables, when they are the results of (A) maximizing welfare of W1 and W2', (B) maximizing welfare of W1 and W3' and (C) maximizing welfare of W1, W2' and W3'. Logarithmic welfare functions. For comparison D gives actual 1975 figures (bn 1975 US$)*

Variables (bn 1975 US$)	A W1W2'	B W1W3' (i)	(ii)	C W1W2'W3'	D
y_1 Non-mil. exp. of W1	3238	1234	1295	1315	3699
y'_2 Non-mil. exp. of W2'	1814	.	.	736	1139
y'_3 Non-mil. exp. of W3'	.	5123	5374	5457	2644
a_1 Milit. exp. of W1	40[1]	167	0	58	167
a'_2 Milit. exp. of W2'	40[1]	.	.	58	113
a'_3 Milit. exp. of W3'	.	145	0	296	145
v'_{12} Security assistance	602	.	.	− 457	0
v'_{13} Developm. assistance	.	2479	2585	2964	14

[1] Chosen equal to value in Table 3.21, also based on logarithmic welfare functions.
(i) Military expenditures of W1 and W3' as in 1975.
(ii) Full disarmament.

Table 3.42 *Optimal values of the variables, when they are the result of (A) maximizing welfare of W1 and W2', (B) maximizing welfare of W1 and W3' and (C) maximizing welfare of W1, W2' and W3'. Parabolic welfare functions, where satiation values are chosen so as to maximize world welfare. For comparison D gives actual 1975 figures (bn 1975US$)*

Variables (bn 1975 US$)	A W1W2'	B W1W3' (i)	(ii)	C W1W2'W3'	D
y_1 Non-mil. exp. of W1	3226	959	997	1344	3699
y'_2 Non-mil. exp. of W2'	1806	.	.	753	1139
y'_3 Non-mil. exp. of W3'	.	3978	4135	5579	2644
a_1 Milit. exp. of W1	50	167	0	50	167
a'_2 Milit. exp. of W2'	50	.	.	50	113
a'_3 Milit. exp. of W3'	.	145	0	145	145
v'_{12} Security assistance	604	.	.	− 449	0
v'_{13} Developm. assistance	.	2871	.	2935	14

(i) Military expenditures of W1 and W3' as in 1975.
(ii) Full disarmament.

Table 3.43 Optimum values of the variables, as shown in Table 3.4 and those obtained by substituting $v_{01} = 0$ for $\alpha = 0.9$ and $\alpha = 0.8$.

Variables (bn 1975 US$)			$\alpha = 0.9$	$\alpha = 0.8$
y_1	Non-mil. exp. of W1	1315	1231	1232
y'_2	Non-mil. exp. of W2'	736	1198	1204
y'_3	Non-mil. exp. of W3'	5457	5108	5112
a_1	Milit. exp. of W1	58	54	48
a'_2	Milit. exp. of W2'	58	54	48
a'_3	Milit. exp. of W3'	296	277	281
v'_{12}	Security assistance	− 457	0	0
v'_{13}	Developm. assistance	2964	2595	2600

carry out the calculation of the optimum values for two values of α, 0.9 and 0.8. Table 3.43 shows the results. Apparently the results are not very sensitive to the values of α and so are rather reliable.

The problem to which this chapter is devoted is, as announced in Section 3.1, whether a relation exists between the policies of disarmament and of development co-operation. The alternative compositions of the Second and the Third Worlds considered in the present chapter centred around the question of whether China should be considered part of the Second or of the Third World. Another approach is to consider China as a world of its own. This possibility will be studied in Chapter 4. For this reason we postpone drawing conclusions until this study has been carried out, that is until the end of Chapter 4.

4. Four-worlds models

4.1 MODELS IN WHICH CHINA IS CONSIDERED AS W4

The unrealistic results obtained in Section 3.4, where China was taken as part of the Third World, constitute an argument in favour of a different model, where China is considered a world of its own called W4. There are convincing arguments in favour of such a procedure. China combines two characteristics, being underdeveloped (as W3) and communist-ruled (as W2'). Moreover, it is less armed than the Soviet Union and, since 1960, is not an ally of the Soviet Union. Its need for development is much stronger than that of the Warsaw Pact countries; and it has its own problems with Taiwan, Vietnam and South-East Asia generally. In the present chapter the optimum values of all variables so far considered for three 'worlds' will now be considered for four 'worlds'. The advantage of doing so is, of course, that the Second and the Third World are now more homogeneous than in Chapter 3. Since in Chapters 2 and 3 we did not obtain very different results using the three alternative welfare functions, we shall only use the logarithmic welfare function. Again the pure Lagrange method to find optimum values will be applied. The coefficients α_{ij} linking welfare and security have been only partly measured which forces our first attempt to use them in our model to be a crude approximation only. Moreover, we shall introduce the 'mixed' coefficients α_{12} and α_{21} only for the First and Second World, since their relevance far surpasses the impact on general security of the relevance of the armament levels of the Third and Fourth World. For the latter, our model will be simpler, and only one-index coefficients α_3 and α_4 will be used to indicate the link between their armament and world welfare-in-security.

The level of security assistance v_{12} will we assumed to be 1 per cent of W1 income, hence 39 billion 1975 US \$. This is done because preparatory studies with a free v_{12} often led to unrealistic results.

4.2   FOUR WORLDS OPTIMUM WITH LOGARITHMIC WELFARE FUNCTIONS

It seems appropriate to spell out in detail how the optima considered in cases A, B and C, as studied in Chapter 3, are defined. In the most general case, C, it is assumed that, by negotiations between the four worlds considered, their governments succeed to agree on the values of all expenditures (non-military y and military a) which maximize total welfare, and on the transfers v_{12} and v_{13} from the First to, respectively, the Second and the Third World necessary to attain that goal. With regard to 'security aid' v_{12} as defined earlier, we assume it will be 1 per cent of the income 3880 bn 1975 US \$, so as to avoid unrealistic values obtained in Section 3.4. This optimum will be obtained by maximizing world welfare Ω:

$$\Omega = \ln(y_1 + 1) + 0.56 \ln (y_2 + 0.56) + 2.85 \ln (y_3 + 2.85) + 1.30 \ln (y_4 + 1.30) + \alpha_{11} \ln (a_1 + 1) - \alpha_{12} \ln (\alpha_2 + 1) + 0.56\alpha_{22}(a_2 + 0.56) - 0.56 \alpha_{12}\ln (a_1 + 0.56) + 2.85 \alpha_3\ln(a_3 + 2.85) + 1.30 \alpha_4\ln(a_4 + 1.30) + \lambda_1(3880 - y_1 - a_1 - 39 - v_{13}) + \lambda_2(1252 - y_2 - a_2 + 39) + \lambda_3(1999 - y_3 - a_3 + v_{13}) + \lambda_4(790 - y_4 - a_4) + \mu(a_1 - a_2)$$

under the restrictions

$$3880 = y_1 + a_1 + 39 + v_{13} \tag{R1}$$
$$1252 = y_2 + a_2 - 39 \tag{R2}$$
$$1999 = y_3 + a_3 - v_{13} \tag{R3}$$
$$790 = y_4 + a_4 \tag{R4}$$

These restrictions are found in the expression for Ω behind the Lagrange multipliers λ_i ($i = 1, 2, 3, 4$). An additional restriction on the armament expenditures a_1 and a_2 is added, namely, that they are equal ('equal strength' of First and Second World).

The maximum conditions are obtained by differentiating Ω with regard to each of the variables and putting these derivatives equal to zero:

$$\frac{1}{y_1 + 1} - \lambda_1 = 0 \quad (4.21) \qquad \frac{\alpha_{11}}{a_1 + 1} - \frac{\alpha_{12}}{a_1 + 0.56} - \lambda_1 - \mu = 0 \tag{4.22}$$

$$\frac{0.56}{y_2 + 1} - \lambda_2 = 0 \quad (4.23) \qquad \frac{-\alpha_{12}}{a_2 + 1} + \frac{\alpha_{22}}{a_2 + 0.56} - \lambda_2 + \mu = 0 \tag{4.24}$$

$$\frac{2.85}{y_3 + 2.85} - \lambda_3 = 0 \quad (4.25) \qquad \frac{2.85\alpha_3}{a_3 + 2.85} - \lambda_3 = 0 \quad (4.26)$$

$$\frac{1.30}{y_3 + 1.30} - \lambda_4 = 0 \quad (4.27) \qquad \frac{1.30\alpha_4}{a_4 + 1.30} - \lambda_4 = 0 \quad (4.28)$$

$$-\lambda_1 + \lambda_3 = 0 \qquad (4.29)$$

We have based our estimates of the coefficients α used on the figures of Table 4 of Appendix II. There we find a figure of 0.043 for the ratio between armament expenditures and real national income for W1, which for us implies that $\alpha_{11} = 0.043$. Similarly, $\alpha_{22} = 0.090$. For the α_{12} we assume it is one-half of α_{22} which means $\alpha_{12} = 0.045$. Similarly, $\alpha_{21} = 0.5\,\alpha_{11} = 0.022$. The values for α_3 and α_4 have been chosen equal to the ratios of armament expenditure to income for W3, hence $\alpha_3 = 0.049$ and $\alpha_4 = 0.083$. All these figures are again halved in order to reflect the impact of the conclusion of an arms reduction agreement. For the solution of the system of equations it appears possible to find the variables for China with the aid of equations (4.27) and (4.28) in which only these variables appear. Together with (R4) they yield

$$y_4 = 790 \quad \text{and} \quad a_4 = 30 \text{ (rounded to units of 1 bn 1975 US \$)}.$$

This would not have been independent of, for instance, the armament expenditures of the superpowers if we had introduced these as co-determinants of China's welfare.

For the W1 and W2 figures we are able to eliminate these referring to W3, and for the solution of y_1, y_2 and $a_1 = a_2 = a$ we find:

$$\frac{0.018}{a + 0.78} = \frac{1}{y_1 + 1} + \frac{0.56}{y_2 + 0.56} \qquad (4.210)$$

Adding up (R1) and (R3) and using (4.25) and (4.26) we find:

$$y_1 = 1490.5 - 0.255\,a \qquad (4.211)$$
$$y_2 = 1291 \quad - \quad a \qquad (4.212)$$

By trial and error we find the solution for *a* and the two *y*s. The complete solution will be shown in Table 4.31.

4.3   THE SEPARATE NEGOTIATIONS ON DISARMAMENT AND DEVELOPMENT W3

In a similar way we shall now determine the partial optimum situations resulting from separate negotiations between W1 and W2 and of those between W1 and W3. The former deal with military expenditures and are aimed at maximum welfare-in-security of W1 and W2. Only the terms in Ω for these two worlds and only the restrictions valid for W1 and W2 will be used. The separate negotiations between W1 and W3 deal with development assistance and only the terms in Ω referring to W1 and W3 are considered. Since the superpowers' military expenditures are not a subject for negotiation in this case, the two extreme values for a_1, 0 and 167, will be considered, and indicated as cases (i) and (ii). Zero, of course, means total disarmament of the superpowers, 167 means maintenance, on both

Table 4.31   Results of negotiations between (A) W1 and W2, (B) W1 and W3 and (C) between all three worlds W1, W2 and W3 to maximize welfare-in-security of the worlds concerned by an appropriate choice of (A) military expenditure and (B) development assistance. In case B(i) the superpowers are supposed to disarm and in Case B (ii) to maintain 1975 level of W1. Amounts rounded to bn 1975 US$ real purchasing power. D: actual 1975 figures

Variable	A	B(i)	B(ii)	C	D
y_1	3316	1433	1411	1407	3699
y_2	1266	.	.	1276	1866
y_3	.	4140	4022	4237	1901
y_4	760	760	760	760	727
a_1	25	0	167	15	167
a_2	25	0	167	15	182
a_3	.	287	297	101	98
a_4	30	30	30	30	30
v_{12}	39	39	39	39	0
v_{13}	.	2428	2302	2339	14

sides, of the 1975 value of W1 armament expenditures (cf. Appendix II, Table 4).
The results of all negotiations are shown in Table 4.31.

4.4 COMPARISON OF THE RESULTS OF SECTIONS 4.2 AND 4.3

As in Chapter 3, we shall now draw conclusions about the impact of separate negotiations on armament and development expenditures. We do this by comparing columns A and B, respectively, with C.

In column A armament expenditures are $ 10 bn higher than in column C. The results obtained in column B strongly depend on what is assumed on military expenditure by the superpowers. If we take the average of B(i) and B(ii), amounting to $ 2365 bn development assistance, this is $ 26 bn more than the figure in column C. For the extremes (i) and (ii), $ 63 bn more or less are obtained. Considering the average of (i) and (ii) as a separate case we may conclude from Table 4.31 that in three out of four cases separate negotiations lead to more armament expenditure or development assistance than is obtained if negotiations about both issues are conducted jointly. As observed, this simply reflects the old truth that a dollar cannot be spent twice.

4.5 SOLVING THE OPTIMALITY PROBLEM OTHERWISE

As mentioned, in many preparatory studies where the amount of security assistance v_{12} was chosen as a free variable which could play its role in the optimization process, unrealistic values for it were found: sometimes high negative values, meaning that W2 would pay security assistance to W1, and sometimes high positive values, which is not very likely either. For this reason a more sophisticated model was studied which saves the possibility of treating v_{12} as a free variable. For the sake of completeness some information is added. In addition to the restrictions already used, an equation was introduced that can be seen as a purchase (or demand) equation of restriction in armament a_2 of W2 and runs:

$$v_{12} = \varphi \left(\frac{113}{a_2} - 1 \right) \qquad (4.51)$$

Here 113 is the value of a_2 in 1975. A reduction in a_2 can be used by W2 to buy some security assistance v_{12}. How much depends on the value of φ, of course. Within a range from 0.5 and 3 it appears that the effect on the other variables in our models is extremely modest.

It seems appropriate to repeat here that our empirical knowledge of the coefficients α_{ij} and α_i ($i = 1, 2$) is very restricted, and the assumptions we made were meant mainly as illustrations of the order of magnitude – both of the coefficients and, of course, of the unknown variables of our main problems. In the latter parts of our book models and variables will be used whose meaning is clear and simple.

4.6   SUMMARY AND CONCLUSIONS OF CHAPTERS 3 AND 4

We are now in a position to summarize the results of Chapters 3 and 4, as announced at the end of Chapter 3.

A clear answer to our main question in these chapters was given by Tables 3.21, 3.22 and 3.23. In all three cases – where varying welfare functions had been used – we got the clear answer that separate negotiations on armament reduction between the superpowers or between W1 and W2 would lead to higher armament expenditures and security assistance than world-wide negotiations. In all three cases we also found that separate negotiations between the First and the Third World would bring considerably more development assistance. In these calculations China was considered as a communist nation and not as an underdeveloped country. In an attempt (Tables 3.41 and 3.42) to consider China as a developing country and not as a communist country, our results became unrealistic, since in the world-wide negotiations the optimum was located at considerably negative values of security assistance. This led us to consider, in Chapter 4, China as separate 'world' (W4). Since China is a very big country, especially when measured by the size of its population, the model changes considerably.

The answers are less outspoken as in Tables 3.21–3.23. The differences between columns (A) and (C) or (B) and (C) in Table 4.31 – which now summarizes our findings – are much smaller than the corresponding differences in Tables 3.21–3.23. But in three out of four cases, column (A) shows higher military expenditures than column (C) and column (B) shows higher development assistance than column (C). The differences are much smaller than in Tables 3.21–3.23, but this also is due to the avoidance, in the models used in Chapter 4, of models supplying excessive figures in security assistance. Our main result cannot deny that a negative relationship between expenditures for armament and expenditures for development exist.

In the later chapters the importance of this relationship is accentuated by the conclusion that the increase needed in development assistance is of the same – very large – order as the desirable reduction in armament expenditure.

5. Twenty-worlds models: income distribution and a related optimum criterion

5.1 NEED FOR MORE DETAIL; INCOME DISTRIBUTION

The models so far discussed divide up the world population and other variables into the smallest number required to analyze our problems, those of development and of security co-operation. The models constitute the 'frontier macro-models': more macro would have meant the 'macroing away' of our problems. To become somewhat more realistic, therefore, requires the introduction of more detail. Since development co-operation in essence constitutes an income distribution policy we propose to concentrate on more detail of income distribution as a first step towards more detail. Thanks to research done by a number of economists, and in particular by Peter Wiles (1978), we are able to introduce deciles into W1 and W3, that is portions of one-tenth of the population of each world. Since W2 plays a subordinate role in development co-operation, this policy is mainly one of W1 and W3. There are data on the income distribution of W2' as well, and we will discuss them, mainly to compare them with the information on W1. Data on W4 (China) are not known to the author. The refinement obtained may contribute to the solution of some of the problems unsolved in the previous chapters. In fact, an alternative criterion of optimality of development assistance will be one of our results.

As in the previous chapters we are not aiming at completeness, but rather at an orientation and a general impression of income distribution in W1, W3 and, partly, of W2'.

5.2   INCOME DISTRIBUTION IN THREE WORLDS: SOME EXAMPLES

A first orientation is given in Table 5.21.

Table 5.21 Some figures on income distribution for W1, W2' and W3

Country	Year	P95/P05	P95/P50	P05/P50
Industrial non-communist countries (W1)				
USA	1950	20.1	3.16	0.24
USA	1974	12.1	2.90	0.16
Canada	1971	12.0	3.00	0.25
United Kingdom	1953/4	5.8	2.51	0.435
United Kingdom	1969	5.9	2.51	0.425
Germany, F.R.	1969	5.7	2.66	0.47
Sweden	1967	6.5	2.31	0.36
Sweden	1971	8.9	2.26	0.25
Italy	1969	11.2	3.31	0.295
Industrial communist countries (W2')				
Bulgaria	1965	3.65	1.745	0.48
Czechoslovakia	1965	4.50	1.90	0.42
Hungary	1967	4.0	2.01	0.50
Hungary	1972	4.3	2.065	0.48
Developing countries (W3)				
India, rural areas	1967/8	8.1	3.22	0.40
India, urban areas	1967/8	11.1	3.76	0.34
India (unw. average)	1967/8	8.7	3.35	0.385

Sources: Industrial countries: Peter Wiles (1978)
India: V. M. Dandekar and N. Rath (1971)
See also Appendix III for the base material.

Since the data shown in Table 5.21 are not available for the Soviet Union, Table 5.22 adds some information which fills this gap.

Both tables show ratios between percentiles, indicated by P*n*, which means the income of the person with the highest income of *n* per cent of the population, counting from the person with the lowest income upward. The figure in Table 5.21 shown for the USA in 1950 under P95/P05, 20.1,

*Table 5.22   Some additional data on income distribution in order to
             compare the Soviet Union with other countries*

Country	Year	P90/P10	P90/P50	P10/P50
USSR	1958	4.08	1.91	0.47
USSR	1967	3.11	1.79	0.58
Hungary	1967	2.99	1.715	0.57
Hungary	1972	3.04	1.73	0.57
United Kingdom	1969	3.93	2.04	0.52
Germany, F.R.	1969	3.83	2.09	0.545

Source: P. Wiles (1978); see also Appendix III.

means that in 1950 the richest person of 95 per cent of the American people
had an income 20.1 times as high as the 'richest' person of 5 per cent with
lowest income. Since the person P95 is the median of the 10 per cent richest
people (with respect to income), we may consider him or her as representative of the upper 10 per cent or 'upper decile' of the population, arranged
according to income. Table 5.21 says, briefly, that in 1950 the upper decile
in the USA was twenty times as rich as the lowest decile (according to
income). In 1974 it was twelve times as well-off. For the other western
countries shown the ratio was lower, even in Italy, and, more amazingly,
in India. The communist countries all show lower ratios than Britain and
Germany.

   Table 5.21 comes closer to reality than Table 5.22, where the ratios are
those between the 90th and 10th percentiles, which may be considered as
representative for the upper and lower fifths of each nation. The differences between the Soviet Union and the other communist countries are not
large.

   As an alternative measure of income inequality two other measures are
shown, the ratio of the upper decile to the median income (P50) and the
ratio of the lowest decile to P50 in Table 5.21 and the ratio of the upper and
lowest 20 per cent to the median income in Table 5.22. In each case they
inform us about the upper and the lower half of the income distribution.
High values of P95/P50 or P90/P50 indicate high inequality, whereas low
values of P05/P50 or P10/P50 indicate high inequality. Roughly speaking
this additional information tells the same story as the first column in both
tables: higher inequality in North America and in Italy than in the UK,

Germany and Sweden, and lower inequality in the communist countries. There are deviations in detail from the first column: Italy shows more inequality in the upper half and less inequality in the lower half of the income distribution than the USA; and Czechoslovakia shows more inequality in the lower half than Germany, etc. Moreover, we should not forget, as Peter Wiles reminds his readers in the title of his paper: the data base is shaky. Even so, the figures give us an impression and do not deviate from the intuitive picture we have. Finally, income distribution is an important feature of a society, but not the only one. Unemployment or freedom of speech are other components of a society's welfare, alcohol or drug consumption are others; so is criminality and the way it is dealt with by a country's police.

Data on income distribution in the Third World are few. Those on India are not data on just one country: they are data on an Asian country, and of the three underdeveloped continents Asia's level of income is lower than Latin America's and higher than Africa's. Of all non-communist developing countries India is by far the largest and, finally, in the world of statistics India excels. In 1982 India's population was 28.5 per cent of all developing countries (excluding China). Thus, Indian figures are more significant than any other figures on one country only. But this still constitutes a somewhat 'shaky data base'.

5.3   INCOME DISTRIBUTION AS ANOTHER CRITERION OF OPTIMALITY

Income distribution is a phenomenon that played a very important role in the world's main controversies, the North–South and the East–West controversy. Whereas the North–South issue is in essence the issue that underdeveloped countries have such low incomes in comparison to developed countries, the East-West issue indirectly originated from the low incomes of workers in comparison to capital owners. Socialism in its various forms – from revolutionary communism to democratic socialism – has been a reaction to the fact of welfare inequality. And the figures given illustrate that, in fact, countries in which socialist parties have some power show less inequality in income than countries where socialist parties are almost non-existent (USA) or where feudalism still has not disappeared (India). Socialist forces may also be too strong, as in the communist world, and there we observe, in recent years, some forms of return to 'capitalist' patterns: giving more power to managers.

Table 5.31   Income distribution in all market economies (W1 + W3) and in W1

(1)	(2)	(3)	(4)	(5)	(6)	(7)	(8)	(9)	(10)
Number of persons (millions)			Income per 74.105m.	Income per 167.83m.	Total inc. of each line $bn (1975)	Decile income (1975)	Percent of Total	Decile Income of W1, percent of Total	Transfer in percent
167.8	167.8		12.0	27.2	27.2	44.6	1.3	2.6	+1.3
167.8	74.1	241.9	17.4	39.5	17.4				
167.8	93.7		17.4	39.5	22.1	64.8	1.9	4.0	+2.1
167.8	148.2	241.9	21.3	48.3	42.7				
167.8	19.6		21.3	48.3	5.6	83.6	2.5	5.4	+2.9
167.8	167.8	241.9	25.0	56.7	56.7				
167.8	54.5		28.9	65.5	21.3				
167.8	113.3		28.9	65.5	44.2	102.2	3.1	6.5	+3.4
167.8	128.6	241.9	33.3	75.7	58.0				
167.8	39.2		33.3	75.7	17.7	126.3	3.8	7.6	+3.8
74.1	167.8	241.9	38.4	87.1	87.1				
74.1	34.9		45.6	103.4	21.5				
167.8	132.9		45.6	103.4	81.9	167.6	5.0	9.1	+4.1
74.1	109.0	241.9	58.1	131.9	85.7				
74.1	58.8		58.1	131.9	46.2	260.4	7.8	10.8	+3.0
74.1	74.1	241.9	65	147	65				
74.1	74.1		100	226	100				
74.1	34.9		104.3	236.7	49.2				
74.1	132.9		104.3	236.7	187.5	396.9	11.9	12.4	+0.5
74.1	74.1	241.9	134	303	134				
74.1	34.9		160	362	75.4				
	39.2		160	362	84.6	694.2	20.8	18.0	−2.8
	74.1	241.9	189	128	189				
	74.1		225	510	225				
	54.3		266	602	195.6				
	19.6		266	602	70.4	1403.4	42.0	23.5	−18.5
	74.1	241.9	307	695	307				
	74.1		445	1008	455				
	74.1		581	1316	581				
Total 2419.0	2419.0				3344	3344	100.0	100.0	0.0

From these arguments an alternative criterion of what constitutes an optimal level of development assistance may be derived. That criterion may be the level of transfers from high-income to low-income groups within the non-communist world, that is, in our symbols W1 + W3. We shall illustrate the estimation of these transfers with the aid of a table for 1970 constructed by Kravis and his collaborators (Kravis *et al.*, 1978). The year 1970 is close to the years to which most of the income distribution data apply and it is the year in which the recommendation was formulated that 0.7 per cent of GNP of the donor countries be made available for 'official development assistance' (ODA). Table 6 of the article quoted informs us about the geographical distribution of population and real incomes over seven parts of the world; this will be the basis of our Chapter 6. There are, however, some printing errors in the column we shall use in the present section. The population of all developed market economies must be 740.45 millions and that of the 'other' market economies (than North America and Europe) 145.43.

The population of the developing market economies is 1678.3 millions and so the deciles contain 167.83 millions each, whereas the deciles of the developed market economies contain 74.105 millions. So we have twenty worlds indeed, but the ten developing deciles have more than twice the size of the ten developed market economies deciles. Incomes *per capita* of the deciles are shown in Appendix III, Tables 1 and 2 and multiplied by a factor so as to let them add up to the total real income 2472 'billion' US dollars with 1975 buying power; and, similarly, to 872 'billion' for the developed and, respectively, the developing countries.

Table 5.3 shows the computation, from the data just described, of the income distribution of W1 and W3 combined (all market economies). Column (1) indicates the twenty deciles' population in the order of their average incomes, shown in columns (4) and (5). In column (4) incomes are given per 74.105 million persons; in column (5) per 167.83 million persons. Consequently the figures in column (5) are 167.83/74.105 = 2.2666 times those of column (4). In column (2) the total population of W1 + W3, 2419.0 millions, is divided into deciles of 241.9 millions, with total incomes shown in column (7). Each decile of W1 + W3 is built up from 2 or more lines, up to 4. The decile incomes in column (7) are obtained by adding up the incomes for the lines, given in column (6). The latter can be obtained in two ways: from column (4) or from column (5), taking into account the line's population size as shown in column (2). Since the upper line has a population of 167.83, its income equals the figure in column (5). Similarly, the last line, having a population of 74.105, has an income equal to that in column (4). Incomes of lines with populations not equal to 167.83 or 74.105 must be obtained by proportional reduction of either the column (4) or the column (5) figure.

Whereas column (7) indicates the absolute amount of income of each decile of W1 + W3, column (8) expresses that income as a percentage of total income 3344 'billion' 1975 USA dollars. Column (9) gives the incomes of each decile if total income 3344 were distributed as in W1. Finally, column (10) shows the differences between columns (9) and (8), and hence the transfers needed to make income distribution in W1 + W3 as unequal as that in W1, that is, less unequal. The transfers needed should be paid by the two highest deciles and amount to 18.5 per cent of total W1 + W3 income for the upper decile and 2.8 per cent for the 9th decile. The total amount of transfers, according to this criterion, should be 21.3 per cent of 3344 'billion' 1975 USA dollars or \$712 bn, constituting 28.8 per cent of W1 income in 1975. Though considerably less than the percentages found as the optimum development assistance in the preceding chapters, it still remains an enormous amount. The explanations given also apply here. The optimum as calculated with the aid of a static model indicates a long-term aim. If a development co-operation policy is followed that, at least, reduces the inequality between W1 and W3, the result of the computations of this chapter will also be a lower amount of optimal assistance. But a precondition remains that indeed inequality will be reduced.

It will be clear that the transfers discussed in this chapter cannot be organized, since the individuals composing each decile are spread over the globe. A practical approach requires that the twenty worlds we consider are organized units. These will be introduced in the next chapter.

REFERENCES

Dandekar, V. M. and N. Rath (1971), *Poverty in India*, (Indian School of Political Economy, Bombay).

Kravis, I. B. *et al.* (1978), 'Real GDP *Per Capita* for More Than One Hundred Countries', *Economic Journal*, vol. 88, pp. 215–42.

Wiles, P. (1978), 'Our Shaky Data Base', in W. Krelle and A. F. Shorrocks (eds), *Personal Income Distribution*, (North Holland: Amsterdam) pp. 167–92.

6. Twenty-worlds models: the optimal geographical distribution of development assistance

6.1 A SIMPLIFIED GEOGRAPHICAL PICTURE OF THE NON-COMMUNIST WORLD

In this chapter the optimal distribution of development assistance over donor countries will be studied.

Development co-operation in the restricted sense as considered in this book is a policy with national governments as policy makers. The number of the world's nations is 159 and their size is very different. A model of intergovernmental development co-operation, in order to be treatable, must work with a smaller number of geographical units. Again we owe to Kravis and his collaborators (Kravis *et al.*, 1978) a collection of figures that enables us to work with twenty geographical units, each with close to 5 per cent of the population of W1 + W3. From Table 6 of their article we derive the survey of Table 6.11.

Table 6.11 Twenty geographical areas with approximately equal populations, 1970

Developed areas Country groups	Population per cent of total		Underdeveloped areas Country groups	Population per cent of total	
North America	9.4	(2)	African	13.6	(3)
European Community	10.4	(2)	Asian	44.6	(9)
Other Europe	4.9	(1)	Latin American	11.2	(2)
Rest of developed world	6.0	(1)			
Total	30.7	(6)		69.4	(14)

Figures in parentheses indicate number of 5 per cent areas used in our simplified geographical picture.

51

It is with satisfactory approximation that the population percentages can be rounded to multiples of 5 per cent: the deviations from such multiples being, respectively, 6, 4, 2, 20, 9, 1 and 2, and the average deviation 4.1 per cent. Below we develop models with twenty areas of 5 per cent of the population of W1 + W3.

6.2 OPTIMAL DEVELOPMENT ASSISTANCE IN A TWENTY-WORLDS MODEL WITH LOGARITHMIC WELFARE FUNCTIONS

Developed areas will be indicated by an index i $(1, 2, \ldots, I)$ and developing areas by an index j $(1, 2, \ldots, J)$, with $I + J = 20$ $\qquad$ (6.21)
Assistance paid will be indicated by v_{i0} and assistance received by v_{0j}; evidently

$$\sum_{i}^{I} v_{io} = \sum_{j}^{J} v_{oj} \qquad (6.22)$$

Further restrictions are:
$$(Ri) \quad x_i = y_i + v_i \qquad i = 1, 2, \ldots, I \qquad (6.23)$$
$$(Rj) \quad x_j = y_j - v_j \qquad j = 1, 2, \ldots, J \qquad (6.24)$$

Maximizing world welfare under the restrictions enumerated then requires the maximization of:

$$\Omega = \sum_i \ln (y_i + 1) + \sum_j \ln (y_j + 1) + \sum_i \lambda_i (x_i - y_i - v_i)$$

$$+ \sum_j \lambda_j (x_j - y_j + v_j) + \mu (\sum_i v_i - \sum_j v_j)$$

The maximum conditions are:

$$1/(y_i + 1) - \lambda_i = 0 \qquad (6.25)$$
$$1/(y_j + 1) - \lambda_j = 0 \qquad (6.26)$$
$$-\lambda_i + \mu = 0 \qquad (6.27)$$
$$\lambda_j - \mu = 0 \qquad (6.28)$$

It follows that all $y_i =$ all $y_j = c$, say.
Addition of all (Ri) and (Rj) then yields:

$$\sum_i x_i + \sum_j x_j = (I + J) c = 20c \qquad (6.29)$$

Table 6.21　Calculation of $y_i = y_j = c$ and of development assistance v_{i0} and v_{0j} for the twenty areas of the non-communist world (in descending order of x_i, x_j), as set out in text, per capita in 1975 US$

Areas	Per cap. product x	v_{i0}, v_{0j}	Total[1] transfers	% of x_i
North America	$x_1 = x_2 = 4708$	3377(= 4708 − 1371)	2 × 3337 = 6674	71
European Community	$x_3 = x_4 = 3185$	1814(= 3185 − 1371)	2 × 1814 = 3628	57
Developed outside Amer. and Eur.	x_5 = 2641	1270(= 2641 − 1371)	1270	41
Other European developed	x_6 = 1913	542(= 1913 − 1371)	541	28
Latin American underdeveloped	$x_7 = x_8 = 1191$	180(= 1371 − 1191)	2 × 180 = 360	
African underdeveloped	x_9 to $x_{11} = 412$	959(= 1371 − 412)	3 × 959 = 2877	
Asian underdeveloped	x_{12} to $x_{20} = 384$	987(= 1371 − 384)	9 × 987 = 8883	

$X + \Sigma x_i + \Sigma x_j = 27414$　　Upper part: donor areas

$c = 27414/20 = 1371$　　Lower part: receiving areas

[1]Total: transfers (donated or received) by all units of 5 per cent of area considered, if each unit is represented by one person. In order to obtain actual total transfers all figures must be multiplied by 5 per cent of 'world' population.

Table 6.22 Calculation of $y_i = y_j = c$ and of development assistance v_{i0} and v_{0j} for the twenty areas of the non-communist world (in descending order of x_i, x_j), in nominal $

Areas	Per cap. product x	v_{i0}, v_{0j}	Total transfers	% of x_i
North America	$x_1 = x_2 = 4705$	3683(= 4705 − 1022)	2 × 3683 = 7368	78 ⎫
European Community	$x_3 = x_4 = 2464$	1442(= 2464 − 1022)	2 × 1442 = 2884	59 ⎬ 65
Developed outside Amer. and Eur.	$x_5 = 1825$	803(= 1825 − 1022)	803	44
Other European developed	$x_6 = 1325$	303(= 1325 − 1022)	$\underline{303}$ 11358	23 ⎭
Latin American underdeveloped	$x_7 = x_8 = 585$	437(= 1022 − 585)	2 × 437 = 874	
African underdeveloped	x_9 to $x_{11} = 176$	846(= 1022 − 176)	3 × 846 = 2538	
Asian underdeveloped	x_{12} to $x_{20} = 139$	883(= 1022 − 139)	$9 \times 883 = \underline{7947}$ 11359	

$X = \sum x_i + \sum x_j = 17488 + 2549 = 20437$ Upper part: donor areas

Lower part: receiving areas

$c = 20437/20 = 1022$

Average percentage of income spent on development assistance: 65

Hence

$$c = \frac{X}{20}$$

where X is total income of W1 + W3.

The development assistance to be given and to be received follows for each i and j from (Ri) and (Rj):

$$v_{i0} = x_1 - c \qquad i = 1, 2, \ldots, I$$
$$v_{0j} = c - x_j \qquad j = 1, 2, \ldots, J$$

The value of I is the number of areas for which $x_i > c$, and the value of J is the number of areas for which $c > x_j$. Their values are unknown *a priori* but follow from the value of c. In Table 6.21 the calculation of c and of the v_{i0} and v_{0j} is shown.

The most important new feature of the development assistance figures found is that they are not equal percentages of national product. The figures on national product are expressed in purchasing power, which is more equitable than using nominal incomes. With nominal incomes the figures of Table 6.21 would have been as indicated in Table 6.22. This would mean a heavier burden on the high-price donor nations and a lower burden on the low-price donor countries.

6.3   PARABOLIC WELFARE FUNCTIONS

Maximum world (W1 + W3) welfare will be obtained if

$$\Omega = \sum_i (y_{oi} - y_i)^2 + \sum_j (y_{oj} - y_j)^2 = 0 \qquad (6.31)$$

under the restrictions:

$$x_i = y_i + v_{i0} \quad (i = 1, 2, \ldots, I) \qquad (I \text{ equations}) \qquad (6.32)$$
$$x_i = y_j - v_{0j} \quad (j = 1, 2, \ldots, J) \qquad (J \text{ equations}) \qquad (6.33)$$
$$\sum v_{i0} = \sum v_{0j} \qquad\qquad\qquad\quad (1 \text{ equation}) \qquad (6.34)$$

Maximum conditions are now:

$$y_{0i} = y_i \quad (i = 1, 2, \ldots, I) \qquad (I \text{ equations}) \qquad (6.35)$$
$$y_{0j} = y_j \quad (j = 1, 2, \ldots, J) \qquad (J \text{ equations}) \qquad (6.36)$$

The number of unknown variables is 60: $20 y_{i0}$ and y_{0j} the satiation values, $20 y_i$ and y_j and $20 v_{i0}$ and v_{0j}. The number of equations so far amounts to 41, leaving us with 19 degrees of freedom. We choose 19 equity equations. In their simplest form, assuming that the degree of schooling of the population of each area is the same, these equity conditions might be

$$y_i = y_j = c \quad \text{for all } i \text{ and } j \qquad \text{(19 equations)}$$

We shall deal with a more sophisticated form below.

The solution of our present version of the optimum problem is obtained by addition of all (6.32) and (6.33), leading to:

$$X = \Sigma x_i + \Sigma x_j = \Sigma y_i \; \Sigma y_j = 20c \qquad (6.37)$$
$$\text{or:} \quad c = X/20 \qquad (6.38)$$

From equations (6.32) and (6.33) we obtain all v_{i0} and v_{0j}.

This solution is identical to the solution of Section 6.2, where welfare functions are logarithmic. Table 6.21 shows this solution.

An alternative solution is obtained if we choose a more sophisticated set of equity conditions, namely:

$$y_i = \eta x_i + \eta_0, \; \eta < 1 \qquad (6.39)$$

This reflects the assumption that populations with a higher production *per capita* must have a higher level of ability, obtained by schooling, experience and scientific research. The value of η has not been estimated, as far as the author knows. Its measurement constitutes an interesting research programme. As an example, to show the consequences it has been assumed that $\eta = 0.3$.

The solution of our optimum problem starts again with the equation (6.37) which now takes the form

$$X = \Sigma x_i + \Sigma x_j = \eta(\Sigma x_i + \Sigma x_j) + 20\,\eta_0$$

and hence

$$(1 - \eta) X = 20\,\eta_0 \qquad (6.310)$$

If $\eta = 0.3$ we find that $\eta_0 = 0.7 \times 27414 = 19190$ and $\eta_0 = 959.5$. Table 6.31 gives the complete solution of this more refined approach.

Table 6.31 Calculation of y_i and y_j and the development assistance variables v_{io} and v_{oj} for the twenty areas of the non-communist world if levels of schooling and research differ

Areas[1]	x	n^2	$0.3x$	$y=\eta_0+0.3x$	$v=x-y$	nv	nx	v/x in %
NA	4708	2	1412	2372	2336	4672	9416	50
EC	3185	2	956	1916	1269	2538	6370	40
OAE	2641	1	792	1752	889	889	2641	34
OE	1913	1	574	1534	379	379	1913	20
LA	1191	2	357	1317	−126	−252		
Af	412	3	124	1084	−672	−2016		
As	384	9	115	1075	−691	−6219		
$X = \Sigma x_i+\Sigma x_j = 27414$; $\eta_o = 959.5$						8478–8487	20340	

[1]See Table 6.21
[2]Number of Areas
[3]Average v as a percentage of x:48

Table 6.31 shows that total transfers donated are equal to total transfers received (within an error by rounding of 0.1 per cent) and that the percentages of income to be transferred by donor countries are considerably lower than in Table 6.21.

It seems interesting to ask what values of η and η_0 would be needed in order to attain as the optimal level of development assistance the wellknown 0.7 per cent of the average donor country. Using the formulae (6.32), (6.33), (6.34), (6.39) and (6.310), we obtain

$$v_{i0} = (1 - \eta)(x_i - X/20)$$
and $\eta_0 = (1 - \eta) X/20$

Requiring that $\Sigma_i v_{i0} = 0.007 \Sigma_i x_i$ we obtain from the x_i in Table 6.21:

$$0.007 = (1 - \eta) \times 0.60$$

which, for the six donor areas, yields:

$v_{10} = v_{20} =$ $0.01167 \times 3337 = 39$, as a percentage of x_i 0.83
$v_{30} = v_{40} =$ $0.01167 \times 1814 = 21$, 0.66
$v_{50} =$ $0.01167 \times 1270 = 15$, 0.57
$v_{60} =$ $0.01167 \times 542 = 6$, 0.28

The figures refer to North America, the European Community, the developed countries outside America and Europe and the other European countries respectively. They illustrate the differentiation of an average of 0.7 per cent development assistance over donor areas with different incomes.

We conclude this chapter with some figures about the actual net flows as a percentage of GNP of official development assistance and of private capital in 1975/7 and in 1986 (last available figures) to developing countries, compiled by the Development Assistance Committee of the Organization of Economic Co-operation and Development (OECD) published in its 1987 Report (OECD, 1988) reproduced here as Table 6.32.

Table 6.32   Net flows (as a percentage of GNP) to developing countries of official development assistance and private capital

	Official development ass.		Private capital	
	1975/7	1986	1975/7	1986
North America				
USA	0.25	0.23	0.47	0.03
Canada	0.50	0.48	0.51	−0.03
European Community				
France	0.60	0.72	0.67	0.43
Germany, F.R.	0.36	0.43	0.78	0.26
Italy	0.10	0.40	0.63	−0.10
Netherlands	0.79	1.01	0.96	0.54
United Kingdom	0.40	0.32	2.23	0.92
Other European countries				
Norway	0.70	1.20	0.57	1.61
Sweden	0.84	0.85	0.58	0.11
Switzerland	0.19	0.30	3.12	0.49
Other continents				
Japan	0.21	0.29	0.25	0.50

Source: OECD, Development Co-operation, 1987 Report (Paris, 1988) pp. 200, 201.

6.4   A FURTHER REFINEMENT OF THE MODEL ON THE DONOR COUNTRIES' SIDE

The method discussed in the preceding sections can be refined relatively easily. It seems interesting to do so in particular for the donor countries' side, in order to find the optimal amounts of development assistance and, in addition, to specify the optimal spreading of the 0.7 per cent figure with more precision. In this section we shall take the large donor countries individually and group the smaller donor countries so as to form areas of 1 per cent of the 'world', i.e. W1 + W3. In contrast we leave the receiving countries as before, and group them by continent. In Table 6.41 the refined model is shown: it contains 14 donor countries or groups of countries and three underdeveloped areas. The units of population each contain 1 per cent of the total population (in 1970). The largest donor country, the USA, consists of 9 units, the second largest, Japan, 4, and the third largest, the Federal Republic of Germany, 3. In addition, the UK, Italy and France consist of two units each, Canada and Spain of one. The remaining donor nations have been grouped into relatively homogeneous groups of about 1 per cent. These groups are (1) the three poorest EC-member countries: Greece, Ireland and Portugal, (2) the Benelux, (3) the Scandinavian countries: Denmark, Finland, Norway and Sweden, (4) two neutral countries (Austria and Switzerland), (5) Australia and New Zealand and (6) Israel and South Africa, a somewhat peculiar remnant. We tried to stay as close as possible to the Kravis *et al.* approach of 1978, the source on which this chapter is mainly based, but some deviations crept in for lack of information or of data. These deviations are minor. Table 6.41 shows the composition of the groups, their population and real income in 1970, expressed, respectively, in millions and in 1975 $. For comparison some of the main figures of the Kravis *et al.* (1978) article have been added. Because of rounding the differences are larger than in our other chapters, but the main structure clearly is close to the Kravis *et al.* structure.

With the aid of these data we are going to make two calculations. First, in Table 6.42, we propose to estimate the optimal amounts to be spent on development assistance, assuming that an equitable redistribution requires that an individual producing x_i may keep for himself $0.4 \, x_i + 0.856$. This implies that she or he must pay a 'tax' $v_{io} = 0.6 \, x_i - 856$, or a marginal tax rate of 0.6 and a 'negative tax' if the income is below 1427. The marginal tax rate is in the neighbourhood of tax systems (including contributions for social security) applied in Europe.

The optimal figures for development assistance again are high, al-

Table 6.41 Composition of the market economy country groups, their
population, in millions and in per cent of total population,
per capita *real income, total income in 1975 US$
purchasing power, for 1970 and some comparable figures
of Kravis* et al. *(1978)*

Countries	Population (000,000)	%	No. of Units	Real income (1975 $) Per cap.	Total	Kravis figures Pop. (m)	%	Inc. p. cap.
USA	206	8.51	9	4758	42,822			
Canada	21	0.89	1	4234	4,234			
North Amer.	227	9.40	10	4706	47,056	226.2	9.4	4708
Germany F.R.	62	2.59	3	3701	11,103			
UK	56	2.31	2	3021	6,042			
Italy	54	2.22	2	2598	5,196			
France	51	2.10	2	3497	6,994			
Spain	33	1.37	1	1917	1,917			
Greece	9 ⎱			1970				
Ireland	3 ⎰ 21*	0.89	1	2198	1,755			
Portugal	10 ⎰			1423				
Belgium	10 ⎱			3338				
Netherlands	13 ⎰ 23	0.95	1	3221	3,289			
Denmark	5 ⎱			3763				
Finland	5 ⎰ 23	0.92	1	3073	3,649			
Norway	5 ⎰			3559				
Sweden	8 ⎰			4372				
Austria	7 ⎱ 14*	0.57	1	2793				
Switzerland	6 ⎰			3787	3,251			
Europe (W)	335	13.87	14	3085	43,196	368.8	15.2	2781
Japan	103	4.27	4	2769	11,076			
Australia	13 ⎱ 15	0.64	1	3611	3,521			
New Zealand	3 ⎰			3059				
Israel	3 ⎱ 24	0.98	1	2788	1,645			
South Africa	21 ⎰			1484				
Non. Amer. Eur	142	5.87	6	2707	16,242	145.4	6.0	2641
Totals Developed	705	29.14	30	3551	106,494	740.5	30.6	3343
Africa			14	412	5,768		13.6	
Asia			45	384	17,280		44.6	
Latin America			11	1191	13,101		11.2	
Underdeveloped			70	516	36,149		69.4	520
'World' W1 + W3			100	1427	142,643		100.0	1383

*Deviations due to rounding

though not as high as obtained in Section 6.2 or, for North America, in Section 6.3. The figures of Table 6.42 indicate what level development assistance would have to have, if the same redistribution were to be applied as is judged desirable inside Western European countries.

The second calculation we made is based on the assumption that development assistance of 0.7 per cent of national income is considered to

Table 6.42 Income per capita x_i of countries, country groups or units, number n_i of units, 'tax' (i.e. development assistance) $v_i =$ $0.6x_i - 856$ per capita, total development assistance n_iv_i and percentage $100 \, v_i/x_i$ for fourteen developed and three developing countries or country groups. Figures in [ ] are total incomes of developed countries by continents

Countries (group)	x_i	n_i	$0.6x_i - 856 = v_i$	n_iv_i	$100 \, v_i/x_i$
USA	4758	9	2855	1999 17991	42.0
Canada	4234	1	2540	1684 1684	39.8
North America	[47056]	10		19675	41.8
Germany F.R.	3701	3	2221	1365 4095	36.9
United Kingdom	3021	2	1813	957 1914	31.7
Italy	2598	2	1559	703 1406	27.1
France	3497	2	2098	1242 2484	35.5
Spain	1917	1	1150	294 294	15.3
Three poorest EC members	1755	1	1053	197 197	11.2
Benelux	3289	1	1973	1117 1117	34.0
Scandinavia	3649	1	2189	1333 1333	36.5
Two neutral Eur. countr.	3251	1	1951	1095 1095	33.7
Europe (Western)	[43196]	14		13935	32.3
Japan	2769	4	1661	805 2415	29.1
Australia & New Zealand	3521	1	2113	1257 1257	35.7
Israel and S. Africa	1645	1	987	131 131	8.0
Non America, Europe	[16242]	6		3803	23.4
Developed world (W1)	[106494]	30		37413	35.1
African developing nations	412	14	247	–609 –8526	
Asian developing nations	384	45	230	–626 –28152	
Lat. Amer. dev. nations	1191	11	715	–141 –1351	
Developing world (W3)		70		–38229	
'World' (W1 + W3)			100	– 816	

be optimal as an average for all donor countries, but distributed over donor countries by a formula

$$v_{io} = 0.0117\, x_i - 16.69 \qquad\qquad (6.41)$$

which follows from the conditions that (i) development assistance is linearly dependent on the donor country's income *per capita*, (ii) the assistance received by the underdeveloped countries is obtained (as a negative income tax) by the same formula, (iii) assistance paid in total equals assistance received in total, and (iv) total assistance equals 0.7 per cent of the donor countries' total income. Table 6.43 shows the results.

Table 6.43 Development assistance to be paid by the fourteen donor countries or country groups, according to the principles set out in the text

Country or country groups	Income	Assistance	Ass. as % of income
USA	42822	350.8	0.82
Canada	4234	32.9	0.78
Germany, F.R.	11103	79.8	0.72
United Kingdom	6042	37.3	0.62
Italy	5196	27.4	0.53
France	6994	48.4	0.69
Spain	1917	5.7	0.30
3 poorest EC members	1755	3.8	0.22
Benelux	3289	21.8	0.66
Scandinavian nations	3649	26.0	0.71
2 neutral Eur. nations	3251	21.4	0.66
Japan	11076	47.1	0.57
Australia and N.Z.	3521	24.5	0.70
Israel and S. Africa	1645	2.6	0.16

Income of donor countries has been approached by the real income *per capita* in 1970, multiplied by the integer number of units mentioned in Table 6.41 and not by the exact number of the population percentage mentioned in that same table. Since the amount of assistance has also been computed in the same way, the assistance expressed as a percentage of income (last column of Table 6.43) is accurate. A weak point is, of course, that the real income figures refer to 1970.

The main result of this second calculation, therefore, is that the

Table 6.44 Actual flows of Official Development Assistance (ODA) in 1986 and 1987 as reported by the Development Assistance Committee (DAC) of the Organization of Economic and Development Co-operation (OECD), expressed as a percentage of GNP (national income) and 'optimal' figures adding up to 0.7 per cent

Country	ODA		'Optimal'	Actual/'Optimal'	
	1986	1987		1986	1987
Australia	0.47	0.33	0.70	0.66	0.47
Austria	0.21	0.17	0.66	0.37	0.26
Belgium	0.49	0.49	0.66	0.72	0.74
Canada	0.48	0.46	0.78	0.62	0.59
Denmark	0.89	0.88	0.71	1.22	1.24
Finland	0.45	0.50	0.71	0.71	0.70
France	0.72*	0.75*	0.69	1.04*	1.09*
Germany, F.R.	0.43	0.39	0.72	0.60	0.54
Ireland	0.28	0.20	0.22	0.68	0.91
Italy	0.40	0.32	0.53	0.75	0.60
Japan	0.29	0.31	0.57	0.51	0.54
Netherlands	1.01	0.98	0.66	1.55	1.48
New Zealand	0.30	0.21	0.70	0.48	0.30
Norway	1.20	1.10	0.71	1.71	1.55
Sweden	0.85	0.85	0.71	1.08	1.20
Switzerland	0.30	0.30	0.66	0.41	0.45
United Kingdom	0.32	0.28	0.62	0.52	0.45
United States	0.23	0.20	0.82	0.28	0.24
Average	0.35	0.34	0.70	0.50	0.49

*Inclusive of French 'Overseas Territories'. If these are excluded, the figures are about 30% lower.

development assistance should not be uniformly 0.7 per cent of national income, but a percentage dependent on the donor country's income *per capita*. The scale to be applied may be a matter for further discussion.

As Table 6.43 shows, this varies from 0.16 per cent for the Israel/South Africa group to 0.82 per cent for the USA. Since the Israel/South Africa group is so heterogeneous, we may add that for Israel alone the percentage should be 0.57. A more homogeneous group is that of the three poorest EC countries and their percentage should be, according to the principle set out, 0.22 per cent. The Scandinavian countries and Australia and New Zealand remain very close to the 0.7 target.

We conclude this section with a comparison between the 1986 and 1987 flows of Official Development Assistance as reported by the Development Assistance Committee (DAC) of OECD and the figures for all individual countries, comparable to those of our Table 6.43, shown in Table 6.44.

The last two columns may be considered as 'scores for good behaviour' in matters of development co-operation. Generally the small countries are scoring better than the larger donor countries, but this does not apply to Switzerland and Austria. The bad score of the USA is related to the heavy defence burden of that superpower.

REFERENCES

Kravis, I. B. *et al.* (1978), 'Real GDP *Per Capita* for More Than One Hundred Countries', *Economic Journal*, vol. 88, pp. 215–42.
OECD (1988), *Development Co-operation*, 1987 Report (OECD, Paris) pp. 200, 201.

7. Dynamic models of development co-operation

7.1 INTRODUCTION

So far we only dealt with static models. In static models all variables are supposed to be constant ('stationary') or to be moved by exogenous forces to which the endogenous variables adapt themselves instantaneously. Their values are optimal in one of the senses discussed, that is, either to maximize world welfare or to attain a given lower level of income inequality. A third alternative sense of optimality will be proposed and discussed in this chapter (see Section 7.6). The welfare functions were chosen differently: we used logarithmic welfare functions which assume absence of satiation and two types of parabolic welfare functions in which satiation occurs.

In dynamic models variables are also changing over time when exogenous variables are constant and such movements of endogenous variables are called endogenous movements. Such movements may be 'cyclical', i.e. change direction in successive time periods, or 'one-sided', i.e. either rise or fall over the whole future. These one-sided movements may be directed towards some equilibrium or away from an equilibrium. Accordingly the equilibrium is called stable in the first case and unstable in the second case. Static models make sense only if the constant value constitutes a stable equilibrium, or if the exogenous movements are the result of an immediate adaptation to a stable equilibrium. Optimality, when defined as a maximum of welfare, in a dynamic model may refer to welfare over a finite period or to welfare over an infinitely long period. Welfare over a period will be considered as the sum of welfare in each time unit (e.g. years) of the period. If an infinitely long period is considered this sum is one of an infinite number of terms. It makes sense only if this sum is a finite figure. This requires that the series of terms is converging by a sufficiently strong decrease of the successive terms. This implies that the successive welfare figures are discounted. The question then arises what rate of discount of future welfare must be chosen on the basis of which criteria. Considering welfare over a finite period in fact also constitutes a form of discounting:

welfare in time units after that period are considered to be irrelevant. One argument in favour of such irrelevance may be uncertainty; another argument may be the finite lifetime of the product about which a decision has to be made or of the decision-makers. The problem of discounting constitutes a well-known and difficult problem which has been dealt with by, among many others, T. C. Koopmans (1970) and M. Inagaki (1970).

In this book only a few of the simplest cases will be analysed. The simplest case evidently is the maximization of welfare in one time unit (for which we take one year) following the time unit in which the decision is made, to be indicated by $t = 1$ and $t = 0$, respectively. This subject will be dealt with theoretically in Section 7.2.

In Section 7.3 concrete figures will be given for all concepts discussed in Section 7.2. In Section 7.4 the time unit chosen will be five or ten years instead of one. In Section 7.5 welfare in more than one time unit will be treated.

In the last section of this chapter an additional, hence a third, alternative criterion of optimality will be discussed that requires a dynamic model and therefore could not be discussed earlier.

7.2.   A ONE-YEAR FUTURE: VARIABLES AND RELATIONS CONSIDERED

A dynamic treatment of our problems requires the distinction of values of the variables in different time units. The time unit considered will be indicated by a suffix t: x meaning 'national' income in year t. The world considered (W1 or W3) will now be indicated by an upper index: x_t^1 and x_t^3 respectively for 'national' income of W1 and W3. As before, we shall also consider y_t^i ($i = 1, 2$) to be defined a bit more specifically, namely as consumption expenditure. Since trade between W1 and W3 will not be considered, net exports – which should be part of y_t^i – are neglected. An essential new variable is z_t^i, gross investment of a world's own resources, hence not of another world's resources. These are financed, in W1, by that world's own savings, which are expressed as a portion s^1 of y_t^1. In W3 there are two sources of financing the investments: (i) that world's own savings $s^3 y_t^3$ and (ii) a portion d of x_t^1, W1 'national' income. In both worlds two relations exist between the variables enumerated. First, a spending equation that for W1 runs:

$$x_t^1 (1 - d) = y_t^1 (1 + s^1) \tag{7.21}$$

The left-hand side are the resources available after dx_t^1 has been made available for development assistance to W3. The right-hand side constitutes consumption y_t^1 plus savings $s^1 y_t^1$.

For W3 the spending equation is:

$$x_t^3 + dx_t^1 = y_t^3 + z_t^3 + dx_t^1 \tag{7.22}$$

The left-hand side are the resources available and the right-hand side contains: (i) consumption y_t^3, (ii) investments financed by W3's own savings, and (iii) investments financed out of development assistance.

The second relation expresses that the increase of production is the result of investments. It equals the product of these investments (the capital input z_{t-1}^i and the output–capital ratio b^i (which is the inverse of the capital–output ratio $1/b^i$) and the effect of technological development cx_{t-1}^i. The gestation period is assumed to be one year. So for W1 we have:

$$x_t^1 - x_t^1 - 1 = b^1 z_{t-1} + cx_{t-1}^1 = b^1 s^1 y_{t-1}^1 + cx_{t-1}^1$$

which can be written:

$$x_t^1 = \left\{ (1+c) + b^1 s^1 (1-d)/(1+s^1) \right\} x_{t-1}^1 = B x_{t-1}^1 \tag{7.23}$$

For W3 we have:

$$x_t^3 = x_{t-1}^3 + b^3 \cdot (s^3 y_{t-1}^3 + dx_{t-1}^1) + cx_{t-1}^3$$

or

$$x_t^3 = x_{t-1}^3 + b^3 \left\{ s^3/(1+s^3) + c \right\} x_{t-1}^3 + b^3 dx_{t-1}^1 =$$
$$(1+s^3)\,(Dx_{t-1}^3 + Ex_{t-1}^1) \tag{7.24}$$

For the welfare functions we need the y_t^i as arguments. They are simple functions of the x_t^i ($i=1,2$):

$$y_t^1 = x_t^1 (1-d)/(1+s^1) = Cx_t^1 \tag{7.25}$$
$$y_t^3 = x_t^3/(1+s^3) = Dx_{t-1}^3 + Ex_{t-1}^1 \tag{7.26}$$

For the reader's convenience we list the capital-letter symbols introduced:

$$B = 1 + c + b^1 s^1 (1-d)/(1+s^1) \tag{7.27}$$
$$C = (1-d)/(1+s^1) \tag{7.28}$$
$$D = (1+c)/(1+s^3) + s^3 b^3/(1+s^3)^2 \tag{7.29}$$

$$E = b^3 d/(1 + s^3) \tag{7.210}$$

The relations enumerated enable us to derive from the initial values x_0^1 and x_0^3 the development over time of all variables, if we know the numerical value of all coefficients b^1, b^3, s^1, s^3 and d. In addition we may solve our main problem, where targets for x_τ^i or y_τ^i are set and d is the unknown rate of development assistance.

7.3 ESTIMATES OF THE COEFFICIENTS INTRODUCED AND THE INITIAL INCOMES

In this section estimates will be presented of the values of the coefficients introduced in Section 7.2. We assume that these coefficients tend to a constant value which we want to know for 1970 as our 'initial year', the year in which the Pearson Commission and the UN Development Planning Commission reported and the UN General Assembly discussed the Second Development Decade (DD II). In order to eliminate random fluctuations in the coefficients' values we considered the period 1960–79 for which important sources were available to us, to be mentioned below.

From the World Bank's *World Development Report 1981* (pp. 136–7) we took the average annual production growth percentages shown below:

	1960–70	1970–9
Low income countries	4.5	4.7
Middle income countries	6.1	5.5
Weighted averages (W3)	5.86	5.38 (weights 1 and 5.6, ratio of 1979 incomes)
	.	.
	.	.
	.	.
Non-comm. industrial countries (W1)	5.1	3.2
Non weighted average of 2 periods		
(W3)		5.62 so growth factor: 1.0562
(W1)		4.15　　　　　　　　　1.0415

Alternative source Kravis *et al.* (1982) yields somewhat rounded growth factors for W3 and W1 of 1.0575 and 1.0430, respectively, meaning a difference between W3 and W1 of 0.0145 as compared to 0.0147 for our figures. Technological progress, measured by its impact on the annual growth factor of production, was taken from Denison (1967), p. 281, where this impact was measured as a residual for nine countries. A minimum figure of 0.76 per cent and a maximum of 1.56 are mentioned. We made alternative calculations using $c = 1.0076$ and $c = 1.0150$.

The initial (i.e. 1970) value of d was calculated as
$$v_0^{13}/x_0^1 = 15.95/2472$$
where 15.95 is taken from the OECD (1988) p. 198, and constitutes the total net flow of financial resources in milliards ('billions' in American terminology) for 1970 in 1970 prices. Since Kravis's (1978) figure of $x_0^1 = 2472$ is measured in 1975 prices, a correction had to be made for inflation between 1970 and 1975. On p. 343 of Kravis, real income *per capita* of industrial market economies in 1970 is indicated to be 5210 in 1975 prices and 3735 in 1970 prices. The inflation over the five years is 1.395. Multiplying 15.95 by that factor yields an initial value $d_0 = 0.0090$. Savings rates in terms of x^i were taken from World Bank (1981) pp. 142–3. For 1970 low-income countries saved 23 per cent and middle-income countries 25 per cent; the weighted average is 24.7 per cent. Industrial countries saved 22 per cent. In terms of y^i these rates become $s^3 = 0.33$ and $s^1 = 0.28$.

For W1 we are now able to estimate b^1, the output–capital ratio, with the aid of equation (7.23); we find $b^1 = 0.1562$ if $c = 0.0076$; the capital–output ratio follows: $1/b^1 = 6.40$ years. Similarly we derive b^3 from (7.24) and obtain $b^3 = 0.1777$ and $1/b^3 = 5.63$ years. Initial income of W1 was mentioned above to be 2472 milliards of 1975 international \$; from the same source (Kravis *et al.*, 1978) we get $x^3 = 872$. We conclude this section with some figures on population growth, taken from World Bank (1981). On pp. 134–5 we find:

Population growth per annum, per cent	1960–70	1970–9
Low-income countries	2.2	2.1
Middle-income countries	2.5	2.4
Weighted average, based on population in 1979, 2260 and 985 respectively	2.3	2.2
Industrial market economies	1.0	0.7

For the period 1960–79 the population growth rate is 1.0085 for W1 and 1.0225 for W3.

Now we are able to present the dynamic equations (7.23) to (7.26) inclusive in numerical form with d as an unknown:

$$x_t^1 = (1.0418 - 0.03417 \ d) \ x_{t-1}^1 \qquad (7.23')$$

$$x_t^3 = 1.0516x_{t-1}^3 + 0.1777dx_{t-1}^1 \qquad (7.24')$$

$$y_t^1 = 0.781(1-d)x_t^1 \qquad (7.25')$$

$$y_t^3 = 0.7907x_{t-1}^3 + 0.1336d \ x_{t-1}^1 \qquad (7.26')$$

With their aid we can numerically extrapolate the development of our main variables for alternative values of development assistance as a portion d of W1 income x^1. Our main application of this extrapolation will be discussed in Section 7.6. To begin with, we may check the equations by the substitution of the actual value of $d = 0.009$. For x^1 and x^3 we find $x_1^1 x_0^1 = 1.0415$, not different from the observed value 1.0415, and $x_1^3 = 917 + 4 = 921 = 1.0562 \times 872$, identical to the observed 1.0562. The check appears to be satisfactory.

A second preliminary application is to show the rates of growth $\dot{x}^1$ and $\dot{x}^3$ of x^1 and x^3 for some arbitrarily chosen values of d:

d	$\dot{x}^1$	$\dot{x}^3$	$\dot{x}^3 - \dot{x}^1$
0.02	1.0411	1.0617	0.0206
0.05	1.0401	1.0768	0.0367
0.10	1.0384	1.1020	0.0636

The last column shows the velocity with which production of W3 overtakes W1. So far, we based our figures on the value of $c = 0.076$, a minimum value. Now we take $c = 0.015$, a maximum. This changes also the values of b^1 and b^3. These now become $b^1 = 0.1221$ and $b^3 = 0.1506$ respectively. The capital–output ratio $1/b^1 = 8.19$ and $1/b^3 = 6.64$, admittedly quite high. The numerical forms of our fundamental four equations (7.23) to (7.26) inclusive now become:

$$x_t^1 = (1.0417 - 0.02671 \ d) \ x_{t-1}^1 \qquad (7.23'')$$

$$x_t^3 = 1.0524 \ x_{t-1}^3 + 0.1506d \ x_{t-1}^1 \qquad (7.24'')$$

$$y_t^1 = 0.781 \ (1-d) \ x_t^1 \qquad (7.25'')$$

$$y_t^3 = 0.9498x_{t-1}^3 + 0.1132d \ x_{t-1}^1 \qquad (7.26'')$$

Substitution of the initial value $d = 0.009$ transforms equations (7.23'') and (7.24'') into $x_{t-1}^1 = 1.0415 \ x_{t-1}^1$ and $x_t^3 = 1.0562 \ x_{t-1}^3$, as observed. Substitution of some other values of d yields:

d	$\overset{.}{x}{}^3$	$\overset{.}{x}{}^1$	$\overset{.}{x}{}^3 - \overset{.}{x}{}^1$
0.02	1.0609	1.0412	0.0197
0.05	1.0737	1.0404	0.0333
0.10	1.0951	1.0390	0.0912

7.4 GESTATION PERIODS OF FIVE AND TEN YEARS

In the dynamic model so far used the meaning of the time unit (of one year) is that it constitutes the length of the gestation period: investments made in year $t-1$ raise production in year t by the amount indicated as the output–capital ratio. (As is well known, the term ratio is misleading: the dimension of the capital–output ratio is time and so far we have referred to it in years. The inverse output–capital ratio has the dimension of one over time.) A capital–output ratio of 6.40 years, as we found for W1, means that for an increase of production by one unit a quantity of capital is needed equal to the production of 6.40 years.

A gestation period of one year is rather low. It is realistic for the production of non-durable products such as grain, vegetables and some fruits. The gestation period of investment in durables is longer, depending on the lifetime of the object. Investment in a ship with a lifetime of twenty years has a gestation period of ten years if no technological development occurs to make the ship obsolete before its technical lifetime. Investment in coffee trees or in cattle also shows a gestation period depending on the economically useful lifetimes of the coffee trees or the cattle.

For these reasons we shall now adapt our dynamic model to average gestation periods of five and ten years. To start with, we take five years. Some of our data will change and some will not. No change will occur in pure ratios such as the savings rates s^i $(i = 1, 3)$ and the portion d of W1 income spent on development assistance. Incomes per time unit will change: initial incomes x_0^1 and x_0^3 become five times what they were before: 12360 and 4360 milliards of \$ with 1975 buying power. Growth rates per time unit must be raised to the fifth power: $\overset{.}{x}{}_o^1 = 1.0415^5 = 1.2255$ and $\overset{.}{x}{}_o^3 = 1.0562^5 = 1.3144$. The growth factor $1 + c$ due to technological development must be changed into $1.0076^5 = 1.03858$, and hence $c = 0.03858$.

The capital–output ratios, whose dimension is time as we stated before, must be recalculated from equations (7.23) and (7.24), respectively, applied to $t = 1$ and the results are $1/b^1 = 1.1597$ or 5.8 years and $1/b^3 = 0.8915$ or 4.5 years; both somewhat lower than our earlier figures and clearly somewhat more realistic.

As a consequence the main equations become:

$$x_t^1 = (1.2272 - 0.18863 \, d) \, x_{t-1}^1 \qquad (7.43)$$

$$x_t^3 = (1.3168 + 3.1790 \, d) \, x_{t-1}^3 \qquad (7.44)$$

$$y_t^1 = 0.781 \, (1-d) \, x_t^1 = (0.9584 - 0.1473 \, d) \, (1-d) \, x_{t-1}^1 \qquad (7.45)$$

$$y_t^3 = (0.9901 + 2.3909 \, d) \, x_{t-1}^3 \qquad (7.46)$$

With the aid of (7.43) and (7.44) the growth rates of x^3 and x^1 and the rates of overtaking over five years may be calculated for some values of d:

d	$\overset{\cdot 3}{x}$	$\overset{\cdot 1}{x}$	$\overset{\cdot 3}{x} - \overset{\cdot 1}{x}$
0.02	1.3804	1.2234	0.1570
0.05	1.4758	1.2178	0.2580
0.10	1.6348	1.2083	0.4265

Subsequently we consider the figures for a gestation period of ten years. Incomes for $t = 0$ now become 24720 and 8720 for W1 and W3 respectively. Growth rates now are the tenth power of the annual growth rates (and the squares of those for a five-year gestation period). We find: $\overset{\cdot 1}{x}_o = 1.5017$, $\overset{\cdot 3}{x}_o = 1.7277$ and $c = 0.07865$. The output–capital and capital–output 'ratios' now turn out to be $b^1 = 1.9515$ and $1/b^1 = 0.5124$, $b^3 = 2.6396$ and $1/b^3 = 0.3788$ and so capital–output 'ratios' become respectively 5.1 and 3.8 years, again more realistic than those found for a five-year gestation period. The main equations change into:

$$x_t^1 = \{1.07865 + 0.4269 \, (1-d)\} x_{t-1}^1 \qquad (7.43')$$

$$x_t^3 = (1.7335 + 7.4832d) \, x_{t-1}^3 \qquad (7.44')$$

$$y_t^1 = 0.781 \, (1-d) \, x_t^1 = \{0.8424 + 0.334 \, (1-d)\} (1-d) x_{t-1}^1 \qquad (7.45')$$

$$y_t^3 = (1.3034 + 5.6264d) \, x_{t-1}^3 \qquad (7.46')$$

With the aid of (7.43') and (7.44') we again illustrate the impact of d on the growth rates x^3 and x^1 and their difference:

d	$\overset{\cdot 3}{x}$	$\overset{\cdot 1}{x}$	$\overset{\cdot 3}{x} - \overset{\cdot 1}{x}$
0.02	1.8832	1.4970	0.3862
0.05	2.1077	1.4842	0.6235
0.10	2.4818	1.4629	1.0189

These differences illustrate the core of our problem, which is how to reduce the income differences between the Third and the First Worlds, to which a possible alternative answer will be given in Section 7.6 as announced before. First, however, in Section 7.5 we complete our set of relations with those needed to estimate welfare over a period longer than one time unit.

7.5 WELFARE OVER A PERIOD LONGER THAN ONE TIME UNIT

In this section, welfare over more than one time unit (i.e. gestation period) will be calculated. We do so in order to illustrate that, with the aid of the relations elaborated, a more satisfactory *theory* of optimal *development* can be achieved, based on our first criterion of optimality, maximal 'world' (W1 + W3) welfare. Since only an illustration is aimed at, we choose a period of two time units of five years each, and show numerical results for time units of one year and a decade respectively.

Welfare over two successive time units of five years for W1 + W3 equals

$$\ln (y_0^1 + 1) + \ln (y_1^1 + 1) + 3.21 \ln(y_0^3 + 3.21) + 3.21 \ln(y_1^3 + 3.21).$$

In order to obtain its numerical value, we have to express them in terms of of x_0^1 and x_0^3, of which the values are known and equal respectively to 12360 and 4360 'billion' dollars with 1975 buying power in the USA. To that end, equations (7.23)–(7.26) inclusive will be applied with the coefficient values for five years as the time unit. These equations are:

$$x_t^1 = (1.2272 - 0.1886\, d)\, x_{t-1}^1 \qquad (7.23')$$

$$x_t^3 = (0.9901 \times 1.33 + 2.835 \times 0.8434\, d)\, x_{t-1}^3 \qquad (7.24')$$

$$y_t^1 = 0.781\, (1-d)\, (1.2272 - 0.1886 d)\, x_{t-1}^1 \qquad (7.25')$$

$$y_t^3 = (0.9901 + 2.3909\, d)\, x_{t-1}^3 \qquad (7.26')$$

Applying them to $t = 1$ we find the following expressions in bn 1975 US$:

$$x_1^1 = 15168 - 2331 \, d$$
$$y_0^1 = 9656 \, (1 - d)$$
$$y_1^1 = (11846 - 1821 \, d) \, (1 - d)$$
$$x_1^3 = 5742 + 10425 \, d$$
$$y_0^3 = 3278$$
$$y_1^3 = 4317 + 7838 \, d$$

With their aid we obtain

$$\Omega = \ln \{9656 \, (1 - d) + 1\} + \ln\{(11846 - 1821d)(1 - d) + 1\} +$$
$$+ \, 3.21 \, \{\ln \, (3278 + 3) + \ln \, (4317 + 7838d + 3)\}$$

In order to find the value of d which maximises Ω we have to put

$$\partial\Omega/\partial d = 0$$

Elaboration and simplifying the fractions occurring in the result we find:

$$\frac{-1}{1-d} + \frac{-1 + 0.2665d}{0.8668 - d + 0.13d^2} + \frac{3.21}{0.5512 + d} = 0$$

This equation is satisfied by $d = 0.37$.

In the same way the other two cases for time units $= 1$ and 10 years have been calculated. In addition, three cases were dealt with where periods $t = 0$ and 1 were replaced by periods $t = 1$ and 2 (for W3 only) since the effects of development co-operation by W1 in period t occur in period $t + 1$. In Table 7.51 the results for all cases described so far are shown, and for comparison purposes those for maximizing Ω over only one time unit are added.

A discussion of the results may start with summing up some of the features of the set of values found for d.

(1)   In the right-hand part, referring to a horizon of one time unit only, the two figures are very close. In the left-hand part they are much more spread and they are spread around the values in the right-hand part.

(2)   Values of d are higher, the longer the gestation period.

Table 7.51 Values of d which maximize welfare in W1 + W3 for the periods specified. Logarithmic welfare functions used

Horizon Gestation period	2 gestation periods			1 gestation period		
	For W1	For W3	d	For W1	For W3	d
One year	$t = 0.1$	$t = 0.1$	*0*	$t = 1$	$t = 1$	0.25
	0.1	1.2	0.42	0	1	0.26
Five years	0.1	0.1	*0.39*	1	1	*0.65*
	0.1	1.2	0.74	0	1	0.63
Ten years	0.1	0.1	*0.50*	1	1	*0.68*
	0.1	1.2	0.78	0	1	0.71

(3) In the cases of identical horizons, printed in italics, longer horizons show lower values of *d*, but in the cases of non-identical horizons, longer horizons show higher values of *d*.

Next, some possible reasons for differences found between *d* values may be discussed. Two forces at work seem to be clear:

(1') If development co-operation investments take a short time (short gestation period) less aid (lower *d*) is needed.
(2') If these investments operate more 'intensively' (high output–capital ratio), less aid (lower *d*) is also needed. Since we found that, expressed in the same time units, b^3 is 0.1777, 0.2243 and 0.2640 respectively for a gestation period of 1, 5 and 10 years the 'intensity' of investment rises with the gestation period. The two forces work in the same direction and are (part of) an explanation of the two effects mentioned.

Thus, features (1) and (2) may be explained. It is less clear what may be the explanation of feature (3). On the one hand, identical horizons seem to be more natural, but, on the other hand, the effect of an investment financed in time unit *t* takes place in time unit *t*+1.

In order to complete the survey of our results, a comparison with those obtained from static models is presented in Table 7.52.

How must we interpret these results? Why are the *d* values found from the dynamic models, especially those assuming low gestation periods, so much lower than the values found for the higher gestation periods?

Table 7.52 Values for development assistance as a percentage of donor countries' income (100d) maximizing welfare of W1 + W3 found from static and dynamic models

Utility functions	Static models with China			Dyn. models with gestat. period		
	in W2	in W3'	as W4	1 yr	5 yrs	10 yrs
Logarithmic	50.6	76.4	66.7	Horizon one gestat. period		
Parabolic I	50.1	75.6	60.5	25.5	64.0	69.5
				Horizon two gestat. periods		
Parabolic II	50.5	67.0	66.5	21.0	56.5	64.0
	3.21	3.41				
Source: Tables	3.22	3.42	4.41		7.51	
	3.23	3.43				

Probably because the target they aim at is maximal welfare for a period in the initial years, when the total production (x^1, x^3) is low. Such modest aims evidently require relatively modest investments.

What we want, however, is maximum welfare over longer periods, and for a gestation period of 5 years and 10 years figures of some 60 per cent for d are needed. This brings us in the neighbourhood of the figures found with the aid of statical models, as shown by Table 7.52. These figures, as we already argued in Chapters 2, 3 and 4, are completely unrealistic. The aim set evidently cannot be attained in the course of the next decade. Before we make an alternative choice some more figures about the impact of d are shown in Table 7.53. This table shows that growth rates of W3 production surpass those of W1 production, but only modestly for low d values. For high values of d, W3 catches up with W1 much more quickly. For values of d up to 0.10 there is a maximum at the 5 years gestation period. The figures for $\dot{x}^1$ and $\dot{x}^3$ differ from those given in Section 7.4, because the time units used there are 5 and 10 years, whereas in Table 7.53 time units are 1 year.

A compromise has to be found between the donor countries' willingness to make available more development assistance dx^1 and the interest of both W3 and W1 in reducing the differences in income and hence welfare to an extent that creates a sizeable perspective for W3 citizens. It is such a compromise that will be proposed and discussed in Section 7.6.

Table 7.53 Annual rates of growth $\dot{x}^3$ and $\dot{x}^1$ of national product of
W3 and W1 for gestation periods of 1, 5 and 10 years and
various values of d, the portion of x^1 made available for
development co-operation

d	1 year			5 years			10 years		
	$\dot{x}^3$	$\dot{x}^1$	$\dot{x}^3 - \dot{x}^1$	$\dot{x}^3$	$\dot{x}^1$	$\dot{x}^3 - \dot{x}^1$	$\dot{x}^3$	$\dot{x}^1$	$\dot{x}^3 - \dot{x}^1$
0.02	1.0617	1.0411	0.0206	1.0691	1.0412	0.0279	1.0653	1.0412	0.0241
0.05	1.0768	1.0401	0.0367	1.0809	1.0402	0.0407	1.0774	1.0403	0.0371
0.10	1.1020	1.0384	0.0636	1.1101	1.0386	0.0715	1.0952	1.0388	0.0564
0.20	1.1524	1.0350	0.1174	1.1432	1.0353	0.1079	1.1244	1.0557	0.0887
0.50	1.3085	1.0247	0.2788	1.2379	1.0253	0.2126	1.1853	1.0260	0.1593
0.75	1.4295	1.0162	0.4133	1.2992	1.0166	0.2826	1.2207	1.0169	0.2038

7.6 A CONCRETE THIRD CRITERION OF OPTI-MALITY OF DEVELOPMENT CO-OPERATION

The concepts of welfare and the question of its measurability are perhaps somewhat too abstract for political discussions, negotiation and decision-making. From the material collected and the calculations made we may derive some less abstract suggestions for another, our third, alternative. As set out earlier, the development during the three decades 1950–80 has been characterized by a virtually immobile world income distribution. From an article by Summers *et al.* (1984) we may derive the simplest evidence about world income distribution by taking the unweighted averages of the Gini coefficients calculated by these authors on the basis of alternative assumptions. These averages are shown in Table 7.61.

This stagnating large income inequality constitutes not only an ethically unacceptable situation, but also a threat to world political stability. Policy-makers are insufficiently aware of the accumulation of tensions as a consequence of this inequality. The only remedy is a change in development co-operation policy that clearly opens up a perspective of reduction of that inequality. During a sufficiently short period for the majority of today's world population to be still alive after its completion the policy target must be a sizeable improvement in incomes of the Third World compared with those of the First World. Its main, although not only, instrument must be development assistance. More concretely we propose

Table 7.61 Unweighted averages of eight estimates of world personal income distribution Gini coefficients

Year	1950	1960	1970	1980
Average	0.6205	0.6063	0.6176	0.6131

Source: Summers *et al.* (1984)

that in twenty years the relative incomes of W3 in comparison to W1 – now about one third – should be doubled. Since doubling in twenty years of any variable requires an average annual increase at a rate of 3.52 per cent, we need, according to Table 7.53, a value of *d* of about 5 per cent. More precise figures can be found in Table 7.62.

Table 7.62 Values of development assistance as a percentage of W1 income (100 d) required for doubling x_3/x_1 in 15, 20 or 30 years

Doubling period (years):		15	20	30
Gestation period:	1 year	7.3	5.0	4.1
	5 years	6.7	4.2	1.8
	10 years	8.0	4.9	2.0

The general conclusion that can be drawn from Table 7.62 is that development assistance of 4 to 5 per cent of national product of W1 countries is needed to produce the perspective mentioned. Even if we in W1 venture to propose thirty years of patience, we still have to treble the 0.7 target. In addition we may have to revise our protective trade policies in order to warrant the marketing of increased production.

The target chosen was a doubling of total incomes compared with total incomes of W1, not income *per capita*. This implies that the responsibility for population growth is left to the peoples and the governments of W3, which we think to be proper.

7.7   EQUITY *VIS-À-VIS* FUTURE GENERATIONS

Another aspect of an equitable distribution of welfare is distribution over present and future generations. Our responsibility for future generations does not stop at our children and grandchildren. All – an infinity of – generations will wish to have a happy family life with at least two children. But there is only a finite quantity of natural resources. If we take too much for present generations, the time may come where resources are so scarce as to press consumption and welfare down to poverty levels again. Is it possible to find a policy to prevent this? In the short-term future, further exploration may add as yet unknown resources to those already discovered. But the fact remains that the total stock of resources is a finite figure. In order to provide, with its help, an infinitely long flow of consumer goods the quantity of resources needed per unit of consumer goods must continually fall. This is conceivable only if technology continues to supply increasing productivity in terms of resources. The possibility of such a solution can best be illustrated by the fact that an infinite geometrical series has a finite sum if it is a falling series. Let the quantity of resources per unit of consumer goods be z and let z fall 4 percent annually. If at time $t = 0$ the value of z was z_0, then for some future time t we have

$$z_t = z_0 \times 0.96^t$$

and the total of resources needed over all future will be:

$$\sum_{0^t}^{\infty} z_0 \, 0.96^t = 25 \, z_0$$

This production programme will be possible if (i) the resources available are equal to 25 times the production in year $t = 0$, and (ii) the technological development can continue forever. For this to happen an active policy of research in the widest sense will be needed. It cannot be certain that the rate of technological development will be maintained.

A constant level of consumer good production implies limitations with regard to both the level of consumption *per capita* and the size of the population. If the world population can be kept constant, a constant level of consumption will be possible, but not, as is currently happening, a rising level of *per capita* consumption. If the population goes on growing, either a higher rate of growth of productivity will be needed or a gradual reduction in consumption *per capita*. A fall in population would enable consumption *per capita* to rise accordingly. Finally, on top of all this we have the task of making resources available to the developing countries, and in greater quantities than so far. An additional rate of growth of some 2 per cent per annum of total world production will be required to meet that aim. Again, it means either a reduction in consumption by the developed countries, or a higher rate of growth in productivity in terms of resource input.

From these examples it will be clear that a satisfactory solution of the problem will not be easy to attain. All we can say is that there are solutions, but the conditions to be fulfilled are heavy. The problem is hardly understood by the majority of the world population. Moreover, the figures we need on available resources are largely non-existent. It would be wise if an international group of experts were created by the Secretary-General of the United Nations to report on this fundamental long-term planning problem.

REFERENCES

Inagaki, M. (1970), *Optimal Economic Growth* (North Holland, Amsterdam).

Koopmans, T. C. (1970), *Scientific Papers*, ed. M. Beckman, C. F. Christ and M. Nerlove (Springer-Verlag, Berlin, Heidelberg and New York).

Kravis, I. B., *et al.* (1978), 'Real GDP *Per Capita* for More Than One Hundred Countries', *Economic Journal*, vol. 88, pp. 215–42, Table 6.

Kravis, I. B., *et al.* (1982), *World Product and Income* (World Bank, Baltimore).

Meadows, D. H. *et al.* (1972), *The Limits to Growth* (Universe Books, New York).

OECD (1988), *Development Co-operation*, 1987 Report (OECD, Paris).

Summers, R., I. B. Kravis and A. Heston (1984), 'Changes in the World Income Distribution', *Journal of Policy Modelling*, vol. 6, pp. 237–69.

World Bank (1981), *World Development Report* (World Bank, Washington).

8. Conclusions and Future Research

8.1 INTRODUCTION

In this concluding chapter we shall summarize the results obtained in the preceding chapters and discuss the subjects to be tackled by future research in order to fill some of the gaps in our present knowledge and understanding. Our results are partly of a scientific character and partly consist of concrete policy proposals. The scientific results will be discussed in the present section, subdivided into the subjects dealt with in the preceding chapters. In Section 8.2 we shall discuss what proposals on security policy we may derive from our analyses. In Section 8.3 our proposals on development co-operation policies will be dealt with. As a starting point for our discussion of desirable future research we shall indicate in Section 8.4 a number of lacunae in our present knowledge and understanding. Future research will then be discussed under two headings: how to fill the gaps in the theories developed and how to fill the gaps in empirical data needed to apply the theories. The theoretical gaps will be dealt with in Section 8.5 and the empirical gaps in Section 8.6.

Our analyses apply to very large areas as units of policymaking: in Chapters 2, 3 and 4 even as large as the First, Second and Third World, with occasionally China as the Fourth World . This highly 'macro' economic type of analysis enables us to describe worldwide policies with the absolute minimum of variables and with correspondingly simple models. Although this is an advantage for expository purposes, it is a source of errors common to all macroeconomic models, and we shall encounter some very obvious errors of this kind. Some of these disadvantages are avoided in the 'less macro' models of Chapters 5 and 6, where twenty units of analysis or policymaking are considered. In particular, in Chapter 6 these units are close to the most important policymaking governments, and in Section 6.4 the actual governments of 1988 appear . In a sense our analyses apply to a future structure of more integrated areas, of which the best example is the European Economic Community. We believe that our analyses help to develop what has been called 'a helicopter view', which is considered to be an important characteristic for managers of large –

mostly transnational – enterprises. It should also be a characteristic of statesmen: that is, great politicians.

Our models deal with some essential features of the two greatest world problems, the East-West or security problem, and the North-South or development problem. Alongside the main instrument of co-operation between North and South, development assistance, we introduce a comparable instrument of security co-operation, called security assistance. But the latter is much less important than other forms of co-operation in security policy, such as the creation of international authorities.

In most of our models the amounts found to be optimal for both development and for security assistance are very large, much larger than today's real figures. In a sense they may be considered unrealistic: in part, correctly so. But in another sense they are a 'token on the wall': their message is that the majority of mankind is underestimating to a dangerous degree the intensity or size of the problem. One way of showing this is that a doubling of the incomes of the Third World relative to the First World would take more than a century if the present rates of growth remained as they have been over the last two completed decades, the 1960s and the 1970s. This means that, humanly speaking, there is no perspective for the Third World. A critic of this formulation may ask why relative incomes of the two Worlds are taken: the absolute figures of Third-World incomes are increasing and may double in the coming two decades. Our answer is that in an increasingly interdependent world, relative incomes rather than absolute incomes are how the poor countries will judge their position. By considering total incomes we are already neglecting the fact that population growth is larger in the Third World than in the First World and that the comparative situation is worse for *per capita* incomes than for total incomes. We are already implicitly assuming that the reduction of population growth will be taken care of by the Third World to a sufficient extent.

The very high figures of development and security assistance which we find to be optimal are an overestimation for various reasons. They are the result of models where no account is taken of differences in productivity and where consequently equity in income distribution is taken to be equal incomes for all. A better criterion of equity must take into account that more productive individuals deserve higher incomes to the extent that they make a bigger effort – but only to that extent. If they work with more physical capital and so are more productive, equity does not entitle them to a higher income. Too little is known of these phenomena, but presumably equity does not require that *per capita* incomes are equal in all parts of the world. So some overestimation of productivity in the Third World may be one reason for the high amounts of development assistance.

Another reason for the high amounts we find to be optimal is the undeniable fact that the total population of the Third World is so large. So even if a modest improvement of per capita income is desirable, the total amount may be – and in fact is – high because of the large numbers of people at stake.

The high amounts of security assistance found in a number of cases is due to the inability to make any distinction between goods and services for general consumption and investment and the particular goods and services used for security aid, such as grain and high-tech goods . This suggests that the optimum implies a sort of income redistribution between the First and the Second World comparable to internal redistribution as a social policy and to the income transfers of the First to the Third World. The communist countries do not want such a form of security assistance – it might be interpreted as a recognition that their social order makes for lower productivity (which is the case). One of Gorbachev's reforms is indeed aimed at eliminating such lower productivity, and he rightly does not want 'charity' from the First World. The cases where this assistance is low are to be preferred.

In Chapter 2, two types of welfare functions are presented, the logarithmic and the parabolic welfare functions, the latter being in two versions and introducing the phenomenon of satiation. It is interesting that the results obtained with the three types of welfare function do not differ greatly, somewhat against our expectations. In fact this supports our results. An interesting feature of the second type of parabolic welfare function – where the satiation levels of the variables are chosen so as to maximize world welfare – is that they leave a number of parameters to be chosen freely . This means that there is a multidimensional infinity of ways to maximize world welfare. This is one of the many subjects for future research .

The main problem dealt with in Chapter 3 is whether there is a relation between armament expenditures and development assistance. This relationship was denied in 1986 by the Reagan administration in their argument for not participating in the conference organized by the United Nations on that relationship. There appears to be a clear relation between armament expenditures and development assistance, as could be expected. The method used in Chapter 3 is to consider security expenditures as the result of negotiations between the First and the Second Worlds, development assistance to be the result of negotiations between the First and the

Third Worlds and to test the hypothetical relationship by imagining negotiations of all three Worlds in which simultaneously both types of transfers would be negotiated. If both types were unrelated, the same amounts should have been arrived at in the simultaneous negotiations as were obtained in the separate negotiations. In fact, in the simultaneous negotiations lower amounts of development assistance were found. Since each dollar of government revenue can only be spent once it seems rather obvious that higher security expenditures lead to lower development assistance. The only theoretical possibility of the contrary view is that citizens would be prepared to pay more taxes to finance the additional expenditures, even as much as 100 per cent. According to our analysis they are not prepared to be so generous.

A not-yet-clarified result of the three-worlds models is that security assistance of the First World to the Second World is positive only if China is considered part of the Second World and not if it is considered part of the Third World. Presumably adding China to the Warsaw Pact countries makes the average income of the Second World so low and the marginal welfare of income so high that this attracts valuable spending assistance to the Second World. In several of the cases studied, security assistance was unrealistically high, as noted before. In various other cases that transfer was small or even nil, and these must be considered to be more realistic. One of these is the model in which armament reduction is 'bought' by a type of demand function for armament reduction dealt with in Section 4. 4.

This brings us to Chapter 4, whose main content is that China is introduced as a 'world' of its own. China's size and particular problems are sufficient reasons to treat it as a 'world' of a particular type, but these particular problems are not represented by new variables, which may be the reason that this model does not eliminate our problem of a negative security assistance. For this reason we assumed here that the maximum of world welfare was a boundary maximum and we chose the value of 39 bn $ for security assistance (1% of GNP of Wl).

As noted, Chapters 5 and 6 are somewhat less macro-economic. In Chapter 5 we introduced twenty 'worlds', but these worlds do not coincide with twenty areas. The inhabitants of the First and the Third Worlds are arranged according to income level and subdivided into ten 'deciles' each, that is, groups of one-tenth of total population. As could be anticipated, income inequality between these deciles is larger in the Third World than in the First World, where social security as well as more education have reduced the previous inequality. We estimated the decile inequality of the combined First and Third Worlds and from it the transfers necessary to reduce that inequality to the First-World inequality. These transfers amount to 29 per cent of First World real income. Its order of magnitude is about half of the development assistance necessary to attain maximum world welfare and may be considered a mid-way station on the path to that final goal. As a theoretical exercise it may have its value, but it cannot be translated into a policy advice: there are no decile authorities. Chapter 6, also dealing with a twenty world model, is more appropriate for policy recommendations. Thanks to work done by Kravis *cum suis* for the World Bank, the non-communist world is subdivided into seven areas each about 5 per cent or a multiple of 5 per cent in size, and world welfare maximum is described by the transfers needed from the four donor areas to the three underdeveloped areas. Again, the high about 60 per cent development assistance flows are found to be optimal if *per capita* income is equalized to characterize the optimum. But if incomes in areas with higher productivity are chosen which are higher than incomes in less productive areas, as a *quid pro quo* for higher efforts, more realistic figures can be obtained. As long as the differences in effort are not known we cannot recommend the optimal policy and transfers. They may fall to the 0.7 level, but we don't know. What we do know is that a 0.7 average must not be uniform for all donor country groups, but must vary between 0.83 for North America, 0.66 for the European Community, 0.57 for the donor countries outside America and Europe and 0.28 for the European countries outside the Community. A model with the individual donor countries or, better, with 1 per cent (percentile) areas is shown in Section 6.4.

Chapter 7 specialized in some features of a dynamic model. Although we returned to two 'worlds' (the First and the Third, respectively) again, we introduced consecutive time units of three different sizes: one year, five years and decades. These units are the gestation periods of the investments made. Growth of production in the two worlds was assumed to have two determinants: investments and technological development. Increase in employment was supposed to be negligible. In areas with a labour surplus it is indeed equipment capacity which determines production.

An alternative model in which population growth is, in the developed countries, a co-determinant of production was added in Section 7.7. In Chapter 7 the central relations derived are those which link the values of the main variables x_t^i and y_t^i ($i = 1, 3$ for the First and the Third World) for any time t to those prevailing at $t - 1$. The policy variable entering in these relations is the portion d which the First World makes available for development assistance. The coefficients linking the variables mentioned depend on the impact of technological progress, for which two extreme values are taken, derived from Denison's work. They also depend on the output–capital ratios in both worlds. Since we are accustomed to think in terms of their inverse, the capital–output ratio, in Table 8.1 the latter are shown for the various values of the gestation periods. In fact, the capital–output 'ratios' are no ratios without dimension; they have the dimension time and are expressed in years in Table 8.11.

Table 8.11   Capital–output 'ratios' in years found for three gestation periods and two coefficients c of technological development

Gestation periods:		1 year	5 years	10 years
$c = 0.0076$	World 1	6.4	5.8	5.1
	World 3	5.6	4.5	3.8
$c = 0.015$	World 1	8.2		
	World 3	6.6		

A figure of 6.4 in this table means that the capital needed to increase annual production by one unit requires a capital investment of 6.4 years of this additional production. The table shows that the capital–output ratio is larger for World 1 than for World 3, smaller for longer gestation periods than for shorter, and larger for higher technological progress than for lower. With the aid of the dynamic equations we estimate the development assistance needed (d, as a portion of First World income x^1) for different 'horizons' and different gestation periods. By the horizon we mean the period over which world welfare is considered. The results were discussed in Section 7.5 and also compared with the results of the static models (Table 7.52).   For short horizons and gestation periods lower values for d have been found (21 to 25 per cent), but for longer horizons and gestation periods values of the same order as found with the static models resulted. Partly the same interpretation applies here too.

The material prepared for the dynamic models enabled us to estimate the application of a third interpretation that may be given to the criterion of optimality, again more concrete than the maximum world welfare criterion. Would it not be a good idea to set as a goal for development the doubling of World 3 income relative to World 1 income in a period of about twenty years? That would give a real perspective, as already noted.

8.2 CONCRETE PROPOSALS RELATING TO SECURITY

In some of our analyses we assumed that military expenditures will be reduced; in others such reduction was part of the result of optimizing world welfare-cum-security. Whereas five years ago such assumptions or recommendations would have been considered too optimistic, today they are considered by many to have a reasonable probability of being realized. The enormous waste of the armament race as well as its dangers are now better understood than before. The heavy burden of military expenditure, especially to the Soviet Union and its allies, keeps down the level of living of these countries and reduces the attractiveness of a socialist society far below what it could be. The low level of unemployment and of income inequality – both of them advantages of a socialist society – are now accompanied by a low level of the quantity and quality of consumer goods supply and Secretary-General Mikhail Gorbachev's reforms will raise both quantity and quality.

Other concrete recommendations on security policies are those about security assistance, and more generally non-military instruments. They have been somewhat over-emphasized because in our models they cannot be separated from income redistribution in general and such a redistribution is not aimed at by either side. But they remain an important part of conceivable security policies. In the few models where a distinction is made between offensive and defensive weapons, a shift to the latter is part of the optimal-welfare solution. In an evaluation of this recommendation it should not be overlooked that research in favour of as yet unknown defensive weapons only contributes to more security if it is done jointly by the two parties, that is, in today's situation, jointly by the superpowers. Otherwise the danger of one of the parties obtaining first-strike capability will remain a threat.

Another way of formulating this need for thorough co-operation is that our models' search for optimal world welfare-cum-security has a 'structural' aspect with regard to the decision-making structure that is implied. A real optimum situation can only be obtained by the existence of world authorities in the fields where world-wide decisions are needed. Such fields are international trade policy and international monetary policy, and a more recent, very important, field is environmental policy. In the first two fields authorities exist: GATT and UNCTAD in the field of trade and the IMF in the field of monetary policy, although their power is not yet adequate. With regard to environmental policy UNEP has no power at all.

For security the situation is hardly any better. This means that the conditions to carry out optimal policies are not fulfilled and the creation of adequate authorities is an implicit proposal following from our analyses. The creation of such authorities is the most important task of our generation. So far we only have a few supranational authorities such as the High Authority of Coal and Steel in the European Community.

8.3   CONCRETE PROPOSALS ON DEVELOPMENT CO-OPERATION

Our analyses clearly confirm what has been said by all experts on the subject since 1961: the situation of the Third World in comparison to the First World remains as unsatisfactory as it was in 1950. No change in world income distribution has occurred. The figure of 0.7 per cent of the First World national income to be spent on public development assistance has only been attained by a few donor countries, and the average attained is about one-half of the 0.7 recommended. Moreover, the 0.7 per cent is lower than any 'optimal' figure we tried to derive from criteria that might appeal to the citizens of the First World and their politicians. In an attempt to avoid criteria that are felt to be too theoretical two other more concrete criteria are proposed. One is to let income inequality in the world at large be reduced to income inequality within the First World itself, and the other is to let relative income of the Third World compared with the First World be doubled in a period of twenty years. In both cases clearly more development assistance than 0.7 per cent is needed: the lowest 'optimal figure' we arrive at being 2 to 5 per cent. Pioneers in this subject have been Dr S. Mansholt, the ex-chairman of the European Commission, and the Swiss churches who suggested 3 per cent – much at variance with what the Swiss government has done so far.

Leading politicians seem blind to the danger of poverty in an increasingly interdependent world. If the burden of armament becomes lower they will hopefully revise their negative attitude. Happily, a new wave of 'Voices in Defence of AID', in Hans Singer's words (Singer, 1988), was under way in 1987 and our findings are in full agreement with this wave. Moreover, the percentage needed is of the same order of magnitude as the reduction in military expenditure discussed today. What results as the best slogan, therefore, is 'reconversion from security to development goods'!

8.4   LACUNAE IN SCIENTIFIC APPROACH

In the last three decades an intensive effort has been made in the study of development by a number of scientific disciplines. Important new knowledge and understanding has been added. Many of the data used in this book are examples of this effort and have enabled us to make a start with the subjects we are dealing with.

In the last decade the study of security policy has picked up pace as a consequence of the acceleration of the armament race. The study and furthering of peace is much older, and traces of it in modern form were visible about a century ago. An important event in this development was the establishment of the International Committee of the Red Cross (1863) by, among others, H. Dunant . Dunant was honoured with the first Nobel Peace Prize in 1901, and the Committee itself received the Prize in 1917. Then there were the Peace Conferences of 1899 and 1907 in The Hague, followed by the building of the Peace Palace. Countervailing forces unfortunately were stronger: World War I started almost immediately after the Peace Palace was finished! Even a Second World War had to be fought before the peace forces began to increase in strength. Scientific activities focusing on peace also found support from the Nobel Foundation when in 1982 Alva Myrdal, whose book 'The Game of Disarmament' (1976) was a beacon, was awarded the Peace Prize. In the meantime, the International Committee of the Red Cross had again been awarded the Peace Prize in 1944 and 1963.

Interest in means of encouraging peace received a considerable boost with the discovery of nuclear energy, which brought a quantum jump in the destructive power at mankind's command. Not only did it increase the volume of scientific work needed to strengthen peace policies, but it also contributed to the scientists' feeling of responsibility in the struggle against warfare as a threat to mankind. The first group of scientists to act was the medical profession. In 1980 International Physicians for the Prevention of Nuclear War, Inc. was established and in 1985 this organization – with about 150000 members – was awarded the Nobel Peace Prize. Both the American and the Russian chairmen spoke on that occasion: Bernard Lown of Harvard University School of Public Health, and Yevgeny Chazov of the USSR Cardiological Institute. The latter, in particular, reminded the audience that physicists, including Albert Einstein, who were the discoverers of nuclear energy, had quickly perceived the disastrous consequence of nuclear war and had warned both

people and politicians that a 'new way of thinking' was needed, particularly in international decision-making.

Other scientists have followed the example of their medical colleagues.
Economists too have a responsibility. The central problem of economic
science is to design an economic policy that maximizes human welfare.
Such a policy, as a matter of course, includes the avoidance of nuclear war
and, in this author's opinion, of all war. Armed forces should remain as a
UN World Police. Since, in the past, economists accepted wars as exogenous phenomena they did not put much research effort into finding out how
war may be avoided. With the recognition of their responsibility for human
welfare – which includes security – an agenda of research becomes evident
and constitutes an enormous lacuna to be filled. A number of good
examples for such an agenda is given in the first document addressed to the
profession by the organisation Economists Against the Arms Race (ECAAR)
in its membership appeal.

The modest attempt in this book to add to this new body of research also
produces a number of lacunae, which will be listed and commented upon
in Sections 8.5 and 8.6.

8.5   LACUNAE IN RESEARCH: THEORETICAL
         LACUNAE

The list and the comments will be presented under the headings 'theoretical' and 'empirical'. No attempt to outline an exhaustive programme will
be made. It is too early for such an ambitious setup.

Perhaps the most important lacuna is the definition of the concept of
security. Authoritative sources such as the handbook on international law
by B.V.A. Röling (1985) or the Report of the Palme Commission (1982)
barely define the concept or comment on it. Security is a 'feeling' or a 'state
of mind' about the possibility of a sovereign nation being attacked and
occupied. At opposite extremes would be, on the one hand, the situation
in a completely integrated world community of nations in which conflicts
between nations are solved in a legal process before a World Court of
Justice – 'complete security' – and, on the other hand, the situation where
one nation is occupied by another nation and disarmed – 'complete
insecurity'.

Between these extremes a large number of intermediate situations are
conceivable, and the set of these intermediate positions may be multidimensional. The number of dimensions depends on the number of mutually

independent characteristics of the conceivable situations. This applies to the extreme as well as to the intermediate situations. The extreme of complete security is characterized by the organizational structure of the world community; for instance, the number of decision-making levels and the procedures of decision-making. The structure also depends on the number of problem categories for which a 'world ministry' exists or on the number of 'ministries' at lower levels, such as the European Community or the United States of America. In the situations between the extremes some of the dimensions of security mentioned by Röling may come in, indicated by him as economic, ideological, enemy and weapon security; the latter two together are also called military security. What we need in principle is, of course, a list of security components satisfying the two conditions that together they constitute the totality of components and that each item on the list excludes all other items. Such lists may either be kept simple and work with a small number of items (macro approach) or try to be complete and work with a large number of items (micro approach). An appropriate scientific strategy is, in this author's opinion, to start with few items and gradually refine the analysis. As an example, armaments may be subdivided into two components – nuclear and conventional, or offensive and defensive – as a macro approach, or be subdivided into all existing and conceivable types, a micro approach. If some weapons are neither completely offensive nor completely defensive, a third category can be added.

Next to security, the concept of instruments of security-aimed policy shows lacunae. In our macro approach we first made a list by distinguishing between military and non-military instruments. Both may be specified by a further listing of components. Some examples on listing armaments were given above. Non-military instruments can be subdivided into existing and non-existing instruments. An existing component is to submit a conflict to the International Court of Justice. A non-existing, but desirable, component is to submit the conflict to the International Court and empower the Court to make a mandatory decision. This example illustrates the thesis that a complete list of instruments should contain all conceivable instruments in order to formulate a complete theory of the solution of conflicts, with the obvious aim of finding the optimal policy of conflict resolution.

8.6   LACUNAE IN RESEARCH: EMPIRICAL LACUNAE

By empirical lacunae we understand lacunae in the measurement of variables and coefficients used in our, or other, models for finding optimal policies. A first example is the measurement of security in the situations studied, with, the aim, among other, of testing the assumptions made on the security, or rather welfare-cum-security, functions: testing, that is, whether logarithmic or parabolic functions give a better fit. A second example is the measurement of the coefficients α_{ii} and α_{ij} in the welfare-cum-security functions used. These are concrete examples meant to illustrate the empirical lacunae in our setup and the future research programmes they entail.

Alongside the subjects of empirical research arises the question about the method or type of empirical research. It may consist of the collection of data, as performed by Ruth Leger Sivard, Kravis and Denison. An important additional method is the public-opinion poll method. We mentioned the research done by Van Praag *cum suis* about the welfare brought about by an individual's or a family's income. Their method will be useful – and, in fact, necessary – for the measurement of welfare-cum-security. The interviews must be preceded by an explanation of the concepts used. The international security of a country as experienced by the interviewee may be defined as in Section 8.5, followed by a proposed scale from 0 to 10, or from 0.0 in ten steps to 1.0, where the highest number stands for complete security and the lowest for complete insecurity. The levels between might be indicated by the usual terms: from very bad, bad, insufficient and so on, to good, very good and excellent (which would mean completely secure); but it is also conceivable that words more adapted to the jargon of security or even military experts could be used. Apart from the aspects (dimensions) of the security concept mentioned in Section 8.5, the circumstances in which, at the time of the interview, the country finds itself will also be relevant. Thus, a citizen of a NATO member country may not feel completely secure because she or he anticipates, with a certain probability and within some future time span, an invasion by a member of the Warsaw Pact. (In 1956 or 1968 one member of the Warsaw Pact was even invaded by other members, but that was long ago.) An example of a different kind is that a citizen of a Central American country may fear an invasion by US-assisted 'contras'. Or a citizen of any country may anticipate a negative judgment from the International Court of Justice. The reasons why an interviewee feels relatively secure could also be the subject of one or more questions.

It goes without saying that the date of the interview must be included. Interviews may be repeated at regular intervals and additional interviews may be carried out after important changes in circumstances. Among the latter could be the signing or the ratification of a new treaty, such as the INF treaty. Hypothetical changes may also be the subject of a security interview.

Again, a factor to be considered about public-opinion polls is whether the participants are experts in the subject dealt with – scholars, or military experts, experts in international relations – or whether they are voters or parliament members, or government members. Sometimes it may be particularly relevant to seek discrepancies between these alternative groups. The scientific strategy to be followed in attempts to fill the lacunae in our research should be the general strategy of scientific development: developing, step by step, a theory of the subject chosen and the necessary empirical information; using the information collected for the verification of the theory and adapting the theory so that it agrees with the empirical information.

The main direction in which this process of scientific development must be extended is to search for a world decision-making structure which will enable mankind to attain complete security and so guarantee the continuation of a living, human society, which is the goal of all attempts to improve and embellish that society.

At the moment of completing this book the author discovered Professor James A. Yunker's article 'A World Economic Equalization Program: Refinements and Sensitivity Analysis', *World Development*, vol. 16 (1988) pp. 921–33. In it he estimates the consequences, for six geographical areas, of a programme in which the countries whose *per capita* consumption is more than half the American figure contribute to a Fund (comparable to the World Bank). Their contribution is a fixed ratio of their surplus of national income over consumption plus military expenditure. Countries whose *per capita* consumption is less than half the American figure receive an amount from the Fund the size of which is determined by the size of their population weighted by the difference between the American and their own *per capita* consumption.

All that remains after the donor countries have paid consumption, military expenditures and development assistance is invested in 'generalized capital', that is, physical and human capital. The amounts received by the poor countries are also invested. The production function for each country is a CES-function, the same for all areas. The capital output ratio is 3 years for all areas. The areas considered are (1) the USA, (2) the other developed countries, (3) upper-middle-income economies plus East European non-market economies, (4) lower-middle-income economies, (5) China and India, and (6) other low-income economies.

The development of all regions is estimated for a 35-year period, both without the operation of the Fund and with it. Without it, *per capita* consumption in the developed countries roughly doubles in 35 years: American *per capita* consumption increases by 91 per cent and the other developed countries show an increase of 129 per cent. With the Fund these figures become 70 per cent and 105 per cent. Without the Fund *per capita* consumption of the poorest countries barely increases in contrast to what is attained – according to this model – by the introduction of the Fund: the poorest region will then attain a level equal to 89 per cent of the USA or 91 per cent of the other developed countries. World inequality would have almost vanished.

The amounts to be transferred by the United States – according to this model – are 3.2 per cent to begin with and, for the 25th year, 4.0 per cent. For the other developed countries these percentages are 2.3 and 5.2 respectively. It is striking that the order of magnitude of these figures is equal to what our 'pragmatic' interpretations of optimal development assistance amount to. The base has been laid for a thorough dialogue between economists and politicians.

Yunker's results compared with ours are considerably more optimistic when we look at the developing world. This is partly due to the production function he chooses for all regions, and probably also to the value of only 3 years given to the capital–output ratio. This and similar discussions may be a useful field of further research.

REFERENCES

Palme, O. *et al.* (1982), *Common Security, A Blueprint for Survival*, by the Independent Commission on Disarmament and Security Issues (Simon and Schuster,) New York.

Röling, B.V.A. (1985), *Volkenrecht en Vrede* [International Law and Peace], Kluwer, Deventer.

Singer, W.H. (1988), 'Lessons of Post-war Development Experience, 1945–1988' in Erasmus University, Rotterdam, 20th anniversary of the Centre for Development Planning, *Dynamics of a Dual World Economy*.

Appendix I Logarithmic welfare function for a community of n individuals

The impact of population size on welfare, dealt with in Section 2.1, will be set out in this Appendix, since the treatment in Section 2.1 may have been confusing and may have interrupted the main train of thought. As we shall see, the impact of population size on welfare is more complicated when population is itself an endogenous variable than when it is considered given. In Section 2.1 and in the main text of this book population is considered given, that is, an exogenous variable.

In the main text the symbols x, y, a, etc., refer to 'worlds' and nations, but not to single individuals. In this Appendix we introduce individuals and their income and non-military expenditures will be written $\bar{x}$ and $\bar{y}$. For members of a community of n individuals $y = \bar{y}n$, when $\bar{y}$ is the same for all members; when they have different $\bar{y}$, this symbol will be used for the average *per capita* $\bar{y}$. Welfare of an individual will be

$$\omega = \ln (\bar{y} + 1).$$

In the notation of the main text this may be written

$$\bar{\omega} = \ln \left(\frac{y}{n} + 1\right) = \ln \left(\frac{y+n}{n}\right) = \ln (y+n) - \ln n$$

For three 'Worlds' 1, 2 and 3 we have:

$$\Omega = n_1 \bar{\omega}_1 + n_2 \bar{\omega}_2 + n_3 \bar{\omega}_3 = n_1 \ln (y_1 + n_1) - n_1 \ln n_1 + n_2 \ln (y_2 + n_2) - n_2 \ln n_2 + n_3 \ln (y_3 + n_3) - n_3 \ln n_3$$

If military expenditures are also introduced, terms with a_1, a_2 must be added. In the expression

$$\Omega = n_1 \ln (y_1 + n_1) + n_2 \ln (y_2 + n_2) + n_3 \ln (y_3 n_3) - n_1 \ln n_1 -$$
$$n_2 \ln n_2 - n_3 \ln n_3 \tag{1}$$

the last three terms are data, if n_1, n_2 and n_3 are given and may be omitted in the process of maximilization of Ω.

Appendix II   Statistical data and sources

In this appendix all data on population size, gross domestic product (GDP) or national income and military expenditures of the countries and 'worlds' (groups of countries) considered, and the sources, are presented.

Table 1   Population of 'worlds' considered

Area	Symbol	1975 Millions	Relat.[3]	1982 Min	Relat.[3]	
Developed market economies	W1	688	1	691	1	
NATO members	W1′	(427)[1]	(0.62)[1]	587	0.85	1
United States of America	US	214[2]	0.31	232	0.34	
Communist-ruled countries	W2	1277	1.85	1388	2.01	
Warsaw Pact members	W2′	382	0.56	380	0.55	0.65
Soviet Union	SU	254[2]	0.37	270	0.39	
Underdeveloped market economies	W3	1960	2.85	2508	3.63	
All underdeveloped nations, incl. China	W3′	2855	4.15	3516	5.09	
China	W4	895	1.30	1008	1.46	
World	W	3925	5.70	4587	6.64	

Sources: 1975 figures: I.B. Kravis *et al., World Product and Income* (Johns Hopkins University Press, Baltimore, London, for the World Bank, 1982) pp. 342–4.

1982 figures: R. Leger Sivard, *World Military and Social Expenditures* World Priorities, Washington, D.C., (1985) p. 35.

Notes: [1]Based on ratio of real GDP of W' and W1.

[2]Source: World Bank Atlas, 1977 (World Bank, Washington D.C.).

[3]Relat.: relative population. Left W1=1; right W1′=1

Table 2   Population of seven areas in the 'world' of non-communist
nations 1970, millions and percentage of 'world' population

Area	millions	per cent
Developed market economies	740.45[1]	30.6
North America	226.20	9.4
Europe	368.82	15.2
EEC	251.48	10.4
Other	117.34	4.9
Other	145.43[1]	6.0
Developing market economies	1678.30	69.4
Africa	329.76	13.6
Asia	1078.62	44.6
America	269.92	11.2
'World' of market economies	2418.75	100.0
World	3696	152.8

Source: I.B. Kravis *et al.*, 'Real GDP *Per Capita* for More than One Hundred Countries',
Economic Journal vol. 88, (1978) p. 204.

Note: [1]These figures are corrected in order to avoid an inconsistency in the published
figures.

Table 3   *Gross domestic product of 'worlds' considered*

Area	Symbol	Real, 1975 1975 $bn	Nominal, 1982 $bn
Developed market economies	W1	3880	7801
NATO members	W1'	2406	6156
United States of America	US	1520[1]	3057
Communist-ruled countries	W2	2042	2387
Warsaw Pact members	W2'	1252	2084
Soviet Union	SU	877	1563
Underdeveloped market economies	W3	1999	2608
All underdeveloped countries, incl. China	W3'	2789	2911
China	W4	790	303
World	W	7921	12797

Sources: 1975: I.B. Kravis *et. al., World Product and Income* (Johns Hopkins University Press, Baltimore and London, for the World Bank, 1982) pp. 342–4.
1982: R. Leger Sivard, *World Military and Social Expenditures* (World Priorities, Washington D.C., 1985) p. 35.

Note: [1]*Source*: World Bank Atlas 1977, (World Bank, Washington D.C.).

Table 4   Military expenditures of 'worlds' considered

Area	Symbol	1975 Real[1]	1982 Nominal	% of GNP
Developed market economies	W1	167	334	4.3
NATO members	W1'	120	311	5.0
United States of America	US	97	196	6.4
Communist-ruled countries	W2	182	212	8.9
Warsaw Pact members	W2'	113	187	9.0
Soviet Union	SU	96	170	10.9[2]
Underdeveloped market economies	W3	98	128	4.9
All underdev. countries, incl. China	W3'	145	153	5.2
China	W4	66	25	8.3
World	W		674	5.3

Sources: 1975 real incomes: I.B. Kravis *et al.*, *World Product and Income* (Johns Hopkins University Press, Baltimore and London, for the World Bank, 1982) pp. 342–4.
Military Expenditures 1982: R. Leger Sivard, *World Military and Social Expenditures* (World Priorities, Washington D.C., 1985) p. 35.

Notes: [1]Figures shown under 'Real' are product of percentages for 1982, multiplied by real GDP for 1975, latest year of data on SU real income.
[2]W. Leonhard estimates this percentage at 25 for 1987 (*Bergedorfer Gesprächskreis*, vol. 84 (1988) p. 25, Bergedorf/Hamburg).

Appendix III Data on income distribution

Table 1 *Calculations of decile incomes, W1 per 74.1 million persons*

	GB 1969	I 1969	D 1969 Per cent of P$_{50}$	'EUR' 1969	USA	W1	W1 $bn '75	W1 % of total income
P$_{05}$	42.5	29.5	47	40	24	32	65	2.6
P$_{15}$	57	45.5	59.1	54	44	49	100	4.0
P$_{25}$	71	61.5	71.2	68	63.5	66	134	5.4
P$_{35}$	82	77	82.7	80.5	78	79	160	6.5
P$_{45}$	94	92	94	93	93	93	189	7.6
(P$_{50}$)	(100)	(100)	(100)	(100)	(100)	(100)	(203)	(8.2)
P$_{55}$	109	111	109	110	111	111	225	9.1
P$_{65}$	129	133	128	130	132	131	226	10.8
P$_{75}$	149	155	146	150	153	151	307	12.4
P$_{85}$	200	243	206	216	221	219	445	18.0
P$_{95}$	251	331	266	283	290	286	581	23.5
Total[1]	1184.5	1278.5	1209	1224	1209.5	1217	2472	100.0

Source: Peter Wiles, 'Our Shaky Data Base' in W. Krelle and A. F. Shorrocks (eds), *Personal Income Distribution*, Proceedings of a Conference held by the International Economic Association, Noordwijk aan Zee, Netherlands (North Holland Publishing Company, Amsterdam, New York, Oxford, 1988) pp. 167–92, esp. p. 191.

Notes: [1]Excluding P$_{90}$
GB: United Kingdom; I: Italy; D: Germany (Fed. Rep.): 'EUR': Europe (Western)

Table 2   *Calculation of decile incomes, W3: Figures for India 1967/8 on consumer expenditure in 1960/1 Rs*

Section of	Rural	Urban	Average	W3, $bn '75 per 167.8m persons	per 74.1 m. persons
0–5	74.8	78.2 ⎫	89.8	27.2	12.0
5–10	102.0	112.4 ⎭			
10–20	126.5	145.7	130.3	39.5	17.4
20–30	153.4	183.3	159.4	48.3	21.3
30–40	179.0	220.1	187.2	56.7	25.0
40–50	205.3	259.5	216.1	65.5	28.9
50–60	236.2	304.4	249.9	75.7	33.3
60–70	269.8	358.9	287.6	87.1	38.4
70–80	316.3	441.6	341.3	103.4	45.6
80–90	399.2	580.2	435.4	131.9	58.1
90–95	514.8	789.8 ⎫	781.3	236.7	104.3
95–100	908.6	1330.0 ⎭			
Total			2878.3	872	384.3

Source: V.M. Dandekar and Nilakantha Rath, *Poverty in India* (Indian School of Political Economy, Bombay, 1971).

Name Index

Subject Index